BRIDGES

and SPANS

Shana Priwer

Cynthia Phillips

Sharpe Focus
an imprint of M.E. Sharpe, Inc.

Sharpe Focus
An imprint of M.E. Sharpe, Inc.
80 Business Park Drive
Armonk, NY 10504
www.sharpe-focus.com

Library of Congress Cataloging-in-Publication Data

Phillips, Cynthia, 1973–
  Bridges and spans / Cynthia Phillips and Shana Priwer.
    p. cm. — (Frameworks)
  Includes bibliographical references and index.
  ISBN 978-0-7656-8120-1 (hardcover : alk. paper)
 1. Bridges—Design and construction—Juvenile literature. 2.
Bridges—History—Juvenile literature. I. Priwer, Shana. II. Title.

TG148.P49 2008
624.2—dc22

                              2007040698

Editor: Peter Mavrikis
Production Manager: Henrietta Toth
Editorial Assistant and Photo Research: Alison Morretta
Program Coordinator: Cathy Prisco
Design: Patrice Sheridan
Line Art: FoxBytes

Printed in Malaysia

9 8 7 6 5 4 3 2 1

PHOTO CREDITS: Cover: Sebun Photo/Getty Images; title page: Altrendo/Getty Images; page 6: Scala/Art Resource, NY; pages 9, 15: Fox Photos/Hulton Archive/Getty Images; pages 10, 11, 25, 26, 33, 36, 49, 50, 51, 52, 55, 57, 64, 80, 86, 96: FoxBytes; pages 11, 13, 42, 52, 54, 71: AFP/Getty Images; page 12: Bridgeman Art Library; page 16: Altrendo/Getty Images; pages 17, 19: Photographer's Choice/Getty Images; pages 18, 32, 67, 68, 76, 78, 81, 82, 94: Getty Images; pages 20, 37, 74, 92: Aurora/Getty Images; page 21: CiStock.com/Sebastian Santa; pages 22, 46, 58, 62, 79, 85, 92, 93, 103: Time Life Pictures/Getty Images; pages 27, 34, 60, 61, 64, 101: Hulton Archive/Getty Images; page 29: First Light/Getty Images; page 30: Robert Harding World Imagery/Getty Images; pages 36, 38, 40, 41, 66: National Geographic/Getty Images; page 41: Stone/Getty Images; page 43: Photonica/Getty Images; page 45: Mapping Specialists; page 72: Library of Congress; page 75: Christian Science Monitor/Getty Images; pages 86, 97, 99, 102: Associated Press; page 89: Art Resource, NY; page 91: Courtesy of Turtle Bay Exploration Park, Redding, Calif.; page 100: ©Dundee Central Library; back cover: Getty Images.

CONTENTS

ABOUT FRAMEWORKS

Architecture has undergone sweeping development since people first constructed shelter. In ancient cultures, most architecture was temporary because it accommodated nomadic populations. As communities began to grow roots, so did their architecture. Whether it was residential, commercial, religious, or civic, structures of permanence slowly appeared on the global landscape.

Over time, specific aesthetics and structural techniques developed in different parts of the world. Advancements in the physical sciences allowed engineers to create increasingly complex works that challenged earlier notions. Temples became more elaborate, buildings grew ever taller, and bridges spanned bodies of water that only boats had dared to cross before. Once science and design crossed paths, there was no turning back.

The goal of the FRAMEWORKS series is to provide insight into the science behind the structures that are part of our everyday lives, from the skills developed by the Egyptians in building pyramids, which paved new paths in the transport and construction of stone structures, to modern-day dams that require the application of advanced hydroelectric technology. Basic concepts in mathematics, physics, and engineering help illustrate the science that supports the creation of increasingly complex structures.

This series assumes no prior knowledge of advanced math and physics, but rather builds the reader's understanding by explaining scientific concepts in common terms, as well as with simple equations. Engaging examples illustrate ideas such as mass, force, speed, and energy. Case studies from real-world projects demonstrate the application of these concepts. Stories of famous structural disasters serve an important purpose in showing how, even for professional architects and engineers, gaining knowledge is an ongoing process.

BRIDGES AND SPANS covers all aspects of bridge design and technology. Starting with the history of the bridge, early methods of crossing rivers are discussed. From here, the main types of bridges are categorized by structural type: suspension, truss, beam, and cable-stayed. Each bridge type is seen as a distinct structural form with its own properties and aesthetic. And don't forget the bridge site! Certain considerations are taken when choosing the precise location for a bridge, and a detailed site survey must be conducted.

The actual construction processes of bridge building vary widely and for the most part depend on the chosen structural type. Steel bridges, for example, require different methods of construction than concrete bridges. Cable-stayed bridges, in which steel cables support the deck, have additional layers of complexity that are addressed in the design stage. All bridges, though, share the fact that various forces affect them. Some loads are permanent, such as the weight of the bridge, while others are temporary and change over time.

However, it is not enough to build a simple pathway. Safety measures such as guardrails and lighting must be incorporated into all aspects of the design. A bridge without adequate lighting, for example, could never be used in the dark.

In addition to the standard types of bridges, a few special-case bridges are presented. Floating bridges and portable bridges, such as those used by the military, require a different approach to science and design. Finally, one of the most important parts of any academic experience is learning from one's mistakes, and bridge designers have made their share. Some of the world's most disastrous bridge failures have taught hard lessons, and the bridge engineering has improved because of these unfortunate failures.

The FRAMEWORKS series provides an entertaining and educational approach to the science of building. Read on to learn about the ways that science literally supports our built environment.

1

HISTORY OF THE BRIDGE

Bridges are a common sight today. We take them for granted as we make our way to school, to work, to a friend's house, and everywhere in between. They have become an integral part of the landscapes in our world and are essential for everyday travel.

However, in the earliest civilizations, spanning a lake or mountain pass was not a simple undertaking. The bridges developed thousands of years ago were barely functional. They were not safe for large groups of people, and drownings because of a failed bridge were not uncommon.

Over time, as people gained knowledge and skill, bridges were aesthetically and scientifically designed, rather than simply being placed where convenient. Engineers eventually considered such things as anchoring, the forces of nature, and the human traffic that would utilize the structure in their designs. Modern materials and construction techniques allowed bridges to be longer, and higher, than was previously possible.

Pons Fabricus, 62 B.C.E., is an example of a typical Roman arched bridge.

As time passed and engineering skills were honed, bridge designers started to have some fun planning the structures. This resulted in the construction of bridges that are sculptural works of art as well as completely functional.

Whether the end result is a complex suspension bridge or a simple concrete causeway, bridge design is an entirely different process today than it was 1,500 years ago.

EARLIEST BRIDGES

Before the invention of steel and concrete, the simplest way to span a short gap was simply to lay a piece of wood across it. Fallen logs were the most likely candidates for early bridges because they were sturdy and readily available. Later, probably in the fifth century B.C.E., bridges became slightly more complicated. Bark was removed from logs to allow for easier passage, and more elaborate wooden bridges consisting of multiple logs and shaped logs were possible.

One of the oldest documented wooden bridges was the Pons Sublicius, built in Rome around 621 B.C.E. Made entirely of wood, it spanned the Tiber River. In Latin, *pons* means bridge, and *sublica* referred to a wooden pick. *Sublicius* could then refer to wooden picks, or pilings, that were driven into the riverbed to support the bridge. Because construction of the Pons Sublicius came under the watchful eye of the papacy, it was well maintained. We have knowledge of this bridge because of contemporary writings, as well as its commemoration on a coin of Antoninus Pius, the Roman emperor from 138 to 161 C.E.

Also used in early civilizations, particularly in tropical regions, were bridges made of twisted vines or ropes. They could span longer distances than logs and were, to some extent, portable, as they could be removed and taken from place to place and were considerably easier to carry than a tree trunk! These simple structures consisted of two pieces of vine or rope: a person walking along the bottom piece held the top one for support. More complicated rope bridges used multiple ropes to construct a horizontal ladder-like bridge, usually with handrails. Such bridges are still used today on some hiking trails and remote locations to allow foot travel across rivers or valleys.

In parts of the world where large stones were prominent, flat rocks were often used to build bridges. There is evidence that stone bridges were built around 1000 B.C.E. One example is the Tarr Steps in Somerset, England.

The Tarr Steps, located in England, shows how early cultures used stones as an alternative to a traditional bridge.

ROMAN AQUEDUCTS

The ancient Romans accomplished a great many feats of engineering, including developments in bridge design. One of the most fascinating Roman contributions in this area was the aqueduct—a structure built to transport water from the surrounding countryside into the towns. This innovation relied on two important technologies: the arch and cement.

An arch is a curved segment of a structure. As used in Roman architecture, an arch consisted of a series of stones placed together to form a curve. The arch shape can span a large gap, and as arched structures use only compressive stress (see Chapter 5 for a more detailed explanation of tension and compression stresses), they are entirely self-supporting.

A Roman arch consists of different types of stones or bricks laid together to form a deliberate pattern. The sloping bricks that butt up against one another to form the arch are called *voussoirs*. The keystone, a specially shaped piece in the center of the arch, provides support for the bricks coming into it from either side.

The other key element to the success of Roman architecture was cement. While many types of arches were self-supporting and did not require a bonding agent (or mortar), most brick structures did need something to help hold them together. To create that bonding agent, the Romans mixed water with limestone and clay. Their formula for the mixture was so successful that modern cement is based on the same agents.

The typical Roman aqueduct (the root word, *aqua*, means water in Latin) was a massive structure that could have three or more levels of arches, with the largest arches on the bottom level. Smaller arches were

Voussoirs are wedge-shaped blocks that are held in place by the larger, more prominent keystone at the top.

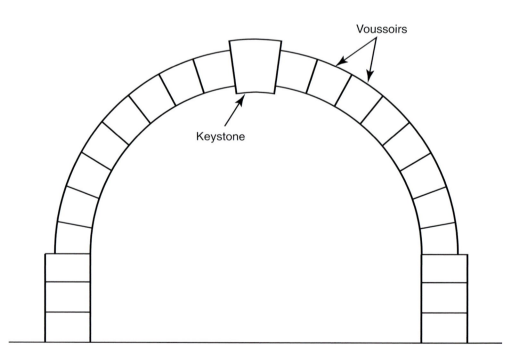

Voussoirs

Keystone

Roman aqueducts, such as this one in Segovia, Spain, appeared throughout the Old World.

sometimes stacked in the upper levels. Since the aqueducts were designed to transport water, a trough-like device called a *sluice* was added to the top level. The sluice had a U-shaped cross-section, and acted like a tiny canal that was open at the top and bounded by stone on the sides and bottom. The sluices were slanted at a very slight angle, allowing water to flow through them to its ultimate destination.

The earliest aqueducts were built in the fourth century B.C.E. By the first century C.E. there were close to 100 aqueducts in Rome, bringing millions of gallons of water a day into the city. Relying simply on the force of gravity, Roman engineers designed simple, yet elegant, systems to bring water into the metropolis of Rome without any mechanical parts.

While aqueducts transported water rather than people or vehicles, they spanned large gaps and served a useful community purpose. In this way, they are true ancestors of the modern arched bridge.

Aqueducts helped transport water into bustling city centers.

MIDDLE AGES AND THE RENAISSANCE

Several hundred years after the Romans, Europeans during the Middle Ages benefited from local building materials and the beginnings of industrialization. One of the major French bridges of the period is the Saint Benezet Bridge, which spans 3,018 feet (920 meters) over the Rhône River in Avignon. Because the Rhône was historically dangerous to cross, this bridge was geographically significant, as it was the only feasible crossing between the Mediterranean Sea and the French city of Lyon. Over the years, the bridge was slowly destroyed by flooding and warfare. "Sur le Pont d'Avignon" is a children's folk song about dancing on the bridge at Avignon.

The Khaju Bridge, in Iran, is an example of an early Islamic aqueduct.

In Florence, Italy, the Ponte Vecchio, which means old bridge, was built in 1345 over the Arno River. Originally built of wood in Roman times, the bridge was formally rebuilt in the fourteenth century under the guidance of Taddeo Gaddi. The massive bridge was constructed of load-bearing masonry using three large arches. This type of bridge is called an inhabited bridge because, in addition to providing a river crossing, it houses shops and other commercial space.

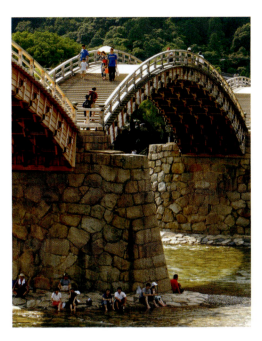

Dating to 1673, Japan's Kintaikyo Bridge is an example of a bridge that uses a combination of wood and stone construction.

The Renaissance brought with it many innovations in architecture, including advances in bridge design. The Santa Trinità Bridge of 1569, also in Florence, was built and rebuilt numerous times over the years. The final version, designed by Bartolomeo Ammannati, was commissioned by the Medici family, who ruled Florence for over 300 years. The elegant, arched stone bridge survived until it was destroyed during World War II, only to be rebuilt once again in the 1950s.

Bridge innovations were, of course, not limited to western Europe. The Khaju Bridge at Isfahan, Iran, dates to 1667 and is one of the most elegant bridges in the early history of Islamic architecture. This bridge uses pointed arches and contains covered passageways that provide shade from the hot sun. Multifunctioning bridges were common in this period, and the Khaju Bridge doubled as a dam.

Another masterpiece of seventeenth-century bridge design is found in Iwakuni, Japan. The Kintaikyo Bridge, built in 1673, has elaborate wooden arches on top of stone piers. The finely crafted wood is far more detailed than any stone bridge of the same period. Japanese craftsmanship is evident in every detail of the Kintaikyo.

IRON AND STEEL

The greatest major structural innovation in bridge design came with the development of new building materials. When iron first became widely used in the 1750s, it had immediate advantages over wood—it would not burn in a fire and could be cast into much longer spans than were possible with a single piece of wood. The Dunlap's Creek Bridge in Brownsville,

Pennsylvania, built in 1839, is one of the oldest American examples of a cast-iron bridge. The flexibility of cast iron also made it possible to embellish structures with intricate details.

There are several other beautiful examples of cast-iron bridges from the Victorian period. The Rio Cobre Bridge in Spanish Town, Jamaica, incorporates cast-iron spans that run between two stone abutments. Interconnecting cast-iron arched segments became a theme that was then applied to other bridges. In a sense, this bridge became a prototype for stone-and-iron bridges everywhere.

Steel was first mass produced in the 1880s by Sir Henry Bessemer, and with steel came the possibility of building very tall—or very long— objects. As skyscrapers quite literally rose to fame in the late nineteenth and early twentieth centuries, bridge design also changed dramatically. Steel lends itself well to the construction of a truss, which is a framework of beams shaped to form a rigid structure.

Truss bridges soon cropped up all over the world, from the United States to England to China, peaking in popularity between 1870 and 1930. Some of the bridges spanning the Allegheny River in Pennsylvania are excellent examples of steel truss bridges still in use today.

APURIMAC CANYON BRIDGE

The Incas of South America used rope bridges to allow traffic to cross gorges and canyons. These bridges were constructed using large anchors on either side of the canyon. Woven grass ropes were then strung between the anchors, with additional ropes used as handholds. The largest of these bridges, the Apurimac Canyon Bridge in Cuzco, Peru, is thought to have been about 220 feet (67 meters) long and was used for centuries by people on foot, and perhaps even riders on horseback.

Early Suspension Bridges

The Menai Bridge of 1826 was one of the world's first suspension bridges. It is located in Wales, part of Great Britain.

Another type of bridge that became increasingly popular in the early 1800s is the suspension bridge. This design, based on the South American rope-bridge design, typically involves suspending the deck of the bridge from vertical cables strung between massive towers. One of the first suspension bridges was the Menai Bridge in Wales, designed by Thomas Telford and completed in 1826. Concrete towers were erected, sixteen cable chains were raised and anchored, and the deck was constructed to complete the bridge. While this bridge was not technically the first suspension bridge, it was both larger and more elegant than any of its predecessors and had a significant influence on future bridge design.

Early Cantilever Bridges

In many geographical locations, anchoring a continuous bridge at two points is not practical. The span might be too long, or the soil unsuitable. The cantilever bridge, developed in the 1880s, allowed bridges to be built under these circumstances. To understand how a cantilever works, imagine a diving board—it is anchored at one end and supports the weight of a person who walks out to the other end. Cantilever bridges use the same anchoring technique.

One of the first cantilever bridges was the Firth of Forth Bridge in Scotland, designed by English civil engineers Benjamin Baker and John Fowler. The strong design of this bridge was in response to a disaster that had occurred in 1879 at a nearby railroad bridge over the Firth of Tay. The Firth of Tay Bridge had collapsed in the wind, killing 75 passengers and crew in a train passing over it. Completed in 1890, the Firth of Forth

BIG MAC

The name "Big Mac" is not solely reserved for a fast-food sandwich! The world's longest suspension bridge, which runs between two anchorages, is the Mackinac Bridge, called Big Mac by those who use it every day. This suspension bridge is located in northern Michigan, connecting the state's upper and lower peninsulas. Since its completion in 1957, the 26,732-foot (7,920-meter) span has been one of the world's longest. The main span of the bridge, located between two towers, measures 3,800 feet (1,158 meters).

Affectionately known as Big Mac, the Mackinac Bridge is a very long suspension bridge in Michigan.

Scotland is home to amazing bridges, such as the Firth of Forth—a pioneering cantilever bridge.

railway bridge was strengthened with an innovative cantilever design that began with two tall towers rising up from the water, each anchored to the bedrock below. From each tower protrude two large steel beams. The beams meet in the middle, and are anchored with diagonal steel tubes. Like a diving board anchored at only one end, the cantilevered design of the bridge allows the steel beams to be supported solely by the towers, resulting in a design that is very strong and secure. The Firth of Forth Bridge, which is almost a tunnel by virtue of its steel-cage frame, was one of the first bridges constructed entirely of steel. In addition to being strong, the bridge looks strong, which helped reassure residents of the area after the Firth of Tay disaster.

One of the first American cantilever bridges was designed by Charles Shaler Smith. The High Bridge, built in 1877, is a railroad bridge that crosses the Kentucky River. With a span of more than 1,100 feet (335 meters) and rising 275 feet (83 meters) above the river, this was one of the highest bridges of its time. It was rebuilt in 1911 and expanded in 1925 to hold two train tracks, and is still in use today.

Rome was not built in a day, and neither was San Francisco's Golden Gate Bridge. Modern feats of engineering depend on the advancements in technology and design that come before them. Without the simple wooden platforms of prehistoric times, the Romans could not have imagined the aqueduct. Without the aqueduct, hefty stone medieval bridges would never have been conceived. And without all of these and other past achievements, modern bridge design would not exist. While the earliest bridges seem simple and perhaps unsophisticated by today's standards, they paved the way for the complex, intricate, and beautiful bridges that grace our landscape today.

GOLDEN GATE BRIDGE

San Francisco's Golden Gate Bridge has become a national landmark. This mammoth suspension bridge crosses the waters between San Francisco and Marin County, California, at the mouth of the San Francisco Bay. The total span of the bridge, including the approaches on each side, measures 8,981 feet (2,737 meters) and the suspended portion of the span measures 6,450 feet (1,966 meters). Like the Brooklyn Bridge, the Golden Gate broke records; it was also the longest suspension bridge of its time upon its completion in 1937.

Before the bridge was built, ferries transported people from San Francisco to Marin County. Engineer Joseph Strauss, the first real advocate for building this bridge, came up with several designs, which he brought to the attention of prominent figures in politics and finance. Because the project was such a massive undertaking, the Golden Gate Highway and Bridge Transportation District was formed to help consolidate aid from several surrounding counties.

The idea took one step closer to becoming reality as Strauss refined his plans in 1929. With the help of engineers Charles Ellis and Leon Moisseiff, he realized that his original design of a cantilever-suspension bridge was simply impractical; out of these discussions came the ultimate design for a full suspension bridge. Unfortunately, the stock market crash and the beginning of the Great Depression also occurred in 1929. During the Great Depression, many people became jobless, and the economic future of the United States was in peril. Fortunately for San Francisco's residents and workers, however, the bridge project was taken on by President Franklin Delano Roosevelt's Works Progress Administration (WPA), which funded large public works to help employ those affected by the Great Depression. WPA workers performed most of the construction tasks on the Golden Gate Bridge project.

The Golden Gate Bridge is the San Francisco Bay Area's preeminent suspension bridge, and averages a clearance over the water of 220 feet (67 meters).

Ellis had worked continually, providing his design expertise for several years. But in 1931, in spite of his contribution to the bridge project, he was dismissed from his engineering firm and removed from the venture. Work continued, and by 1933, construction had begun. Excavation for the anchorages was one of the first jobs. Reinforced concrete anchorages were then constructed on each side of the bay. These huge underground concrete structures served to terminate and secure the massive bridge cables.

Piers, towers, and trestles were added, and by 1934, the north tower was finished. The south tower was completed the following year. A catwalk was constructed in 1935 so that workers could hang cables. Strauss apparently prescribed a specific diet for his catwalk workers so that they would not succumb to catwalk-related dizziness from their perches high above the waters of the bay. Installation and spinning of the suspension cables came next. Steel was laid for the deck in 1936, and the road surface was put in place by 1937. The surface was hung from the cables with 254 vertical suspenders.

Irving Morrow, a Bay Area architect, designed the architectural elements of the bridge. His major contributions are evident to all who pass over the Golden Gate. His design for the style and towers of the bridge was influenced by art deco, which was popular in the 1920s and 1930s and is characterized by bold outlines and geometric shapes. The striking color, called International Orange, helps make the bridge more visible in the pervasive San Francisco

The cables integrated into the Golden Gate Bridge's support system are comprised of 27,572 individual wire strands, which, if laid end to end, would span 80,000 miles (129,000 km)!

fog. Morrow also worked on the lighting design, which contributes to the bridge's astounding beauty.

The Golden Gate project was innovative down to the last detail. For instance, a precursor to the hard hat, developed by Edward Bullard, was given to each worker in the hopes of preventing worker injuries. A massive safety net was also hung beneath the bridge deck, which saved many lives. However, twelve people died during construction of the Golden Gate Bridge, but this relatively low number was celebrated as a construction achievement. One worker was crushed to death by a falling beam, and the others fell through the safety net when a platform collapsed.

TYPES OF BRIDGES

Different circumstances call for different types of bridges. Some span long gaps, some support several decks for traffic, some are useful for curving mountain passes, and some use cables for both strength and elegance. Many types of bridges can be built with either long or short spans. A short-span bridge is generally defined as one that only requires structures at each end, called abutments, for support. When the gap being spanned is too long for this type of bridge, vertical structures, or piers, are placed somewhere in the middle. This type of bridge, with one or more piers, is called a long-span bridge. All types vary in size, length, and weight, and some types of bridges are better suited for long spans than others. This chapter discusses four major bridge types: arch bridges, suspension bridges, truss bridges, and beam bridges.

The New River Gorge Bridge, in West Virginia, is one of the world's longest arch bridges.

ARCH BRIDGES

The arch bridge is an ancient yet elegant design. It typically has stone abutments at each end, with one or more arches in between. Multiple-arch bridges, such as those used in Roman aqueducts, date from ancient times, while single-arch bridges were common in eighteenth-century Europe.

Bridges come in many different types, are created using a range of different materials, and utilize innovative technologies and support mechanisms. Pictured is the Hohenzollern Bridge in Germany, a steel bridge using arched construction.

A bridge must be strong enough to support the loads acting on it. These loads include both live and static loads. Static loads are permanent, and consist of the weight of the bridge and its permanent fixtures. Live loads can vary from day to day and minute to minute, and include forces from the weight of the cars and people crossing the bridge, as well as the forces of nature, such as wind.

Arch bridges work on the same principle as a simple arch: the loads of the bridge are transferred horizontally into the abutments at each end of the bridge. Arch bridges are typically built using full-scale wooden forms, called falsework. Wooden arches are built and raised into position simultaneously. If built in sequence, the arches would exert horizontal forces that would push neighboring arches out of position. Permanent stone arches are then built around the wooden frames.

Early arch bridges were constructed of stone and mortar. After building over the wooden frame, a keystone would be placed at the top to hold the arch together. Modern arch bridges are usually built of reinforced concrete or steel.

Arch bridges can span gaps as small as 100 feet (30 meters) and as large as 1,800 feet (548 meters) in a single arch. One of the longest arch bridges in the world is the New River Gorge Bridge in West Virginia. Spanning 1,710 feet (518 meters), the bridge was built using steel trusses. A long-span bridge made of multiple arches is the Stone Arch Bridge, built in 1883 over the Mississippi River, which spans 2,100 feet (640 meters) and consists of 23 arches. The Landwasser Viaduct in the Swiss Alps is a very high railroad bridge built in 1902. It has six arches, each of which spans 65 feet (19 meters), and the deck of the bridge stands nearly 200 feet (60 meters) above the valley.

SUSPENSION BRIDGES

Suspension bridges have also been around for thousands of years. The main idea behind a suspension bridge is that the load of the bridge is suspended between two or more points. In a typical suspension bridge, there are two or more large towers with curving cables stretched between them. Vertical cables are then hung from the curving cables, suspending the deck.

One major advantage of the suspension bridge over the arch bridge is that it can span much farther. Most suspension-bridge spans are between 230 feet (70 meters) and 3,280 feet (1,000 meters), almost twice as long as the average span of an arch bridge.

Most suspension bridges involve a continuous girder, which is a horizontal beam that supports the loads acting on the bridge, with two or more towers placed along the span. Although made of shorter pieces, the continuous girder acts as one single structural member. The girder is anchored at each end of the span, and cables are strung from one anchor to a tower, to the next tower, and finally to the opposite anchor. Vertical cables are then attached that connect the main cables to the deck as a means of support. One of the world's longest suspension bridges is the Akashi Kaikyo Bridge in Japan. This bridge spans 6,532 feet (1,991 meters) and took about 10 years to build at a cost of about ¥500 billion ($3.6 billion). It serves as part of a connection between two islands, and is enormous in scale. The deck is a trussed girder measuring 46 by 115 feet (14 by 35 meters). The designers also had to maintain clearance of at least 213 feet (65 meters) for tall ships and had to take into account wind speeds of up to 180 miles per hour (290 kilometers per hour). The suspension cables for this bridge—127 wires per cable strand, 290 strands per final cable— were compressed with a machine designed specifically for the construction of this bridge. While bridge cables are usually strung together off-site, in this case they were fabricated in smaller pieces elsewhere and then strung together at the building site.

TRUSS BRIDGES

Truss bridges—first built around 1850—are relative newcomers to the world of bridge design and have several advantages over others. A truss is a particularly stable form that is able to handle tension and compression loads equally well, and comes with an established aesthetic. Trusses are stable forms because they consist of straight pieces of material configured in such a way that they are capable of carrying loads. Different members carry tension and compression forces, providing the main source of struc-

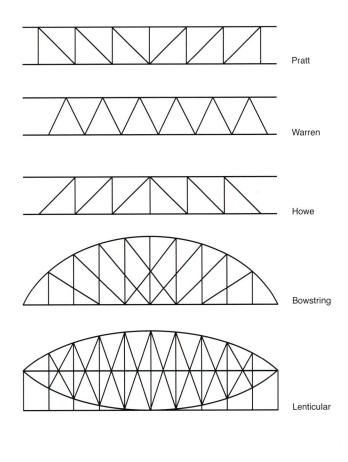

Pratt

Warren

Howe

Bowstring

Lenticular

tural support for the bridge. The arrangement of members in the truss, plus its hinged connections that allow for some flexibility, gives the truss its stability. Typical truss bridges can span between 120 and 1,500 feet (36 and 457 meters).

Steel and iron were key requirements in building truss bridges, since they have a far superior ability to resist tension forces than that of concrete. While cast iron and wrought iron had been available for centuries, changes to the steel-making process allowed the use of steel on a much larger scale than had been possible before. The scientific analysis of the truss and subsequent appreciation of its benefits reached new heights in the mid-nineteenth century, and truss bridges soon proliferated.

A truss bridge, at its simplest, is supported by long pieces made up of steel beams arranged in rectangles with criss-crossing diagonal bars bracing their interiors. Sometimes the truss is underneath, with a road surface on the top. Sometimes the truss makes up the two sides of the bridge, with a road surface at the bottom and an open top. Sometimes the truss bridge is more like a tunnel or a tube, completely enclosing the roadway. Truss bridge design and construction methods vary depending on the material, configuration, and span. Large, complex steel bridge trusses may be fabricated off-site and then installed on-site. A less complex truss bridge, such as a small railway bridge, may be completely assembled on-site.

There are a number of different configurations of truss bridges. The difference lies in the configuration of the bars across the span. One of the most common types of bridge trusses is the Warren truss. With shorter lengths, Warren trusses typically use only diagonal, rather than vertical, bars. For longer spans that require additional support, vertical bars can be added.

The bowstring truss was a popular design in the 1850s. This design involved crossing diagonal bars separated by vertical bars, which created a series of triangle shapes. One example of this bridge type is the Whipple Bowstring Truss Bridge, located in Coschocton County, Ohio. It was patented by Squire Whipple in 1841 and widely used throughout New York State and elsewhere in the country during the second half of the nineteenth century. The innovative design used cast iron for the components of the bridge under compression, and wrought iron for the pieces under tension.

The Pratt truss has diagonal bars that, except for those at either end, slant toward the center of the truss. As with most truss types, the vertical bars at the ends are subject to compression forces, while the diagonal bars receive only tension forces. The Howe truss, designed as the opposite of a Pratt truss, has diagonal bars that slant away from the center and accept compression forces, which makes it a poor choice for most bridges.

Another factor that is taken into account when designing truss bridges, as well as any other type of bridge, is camber, which is the positive, or upward, curve in the bridge deck. By arching the deck of the bridge slightly upward, the weight of the bridge and the traffic crossing it cause the roadway to bend down into a horizontal surface. Camber thus helps to offset the sagging that would otherwise result from the weight of the bridge and its loads.

Camber, or the upward curve designed into bridge decks, helps provide a flat and stable bridge surface once construction is completed.

The Pont de Quebec, or Quebec Bridge, is one of the world's largest cantilever-truss bridges, spanning about 1,800 feet (550 meters). Begun in 1900, it had a disastrous collapse in 1907 midway through construction. One of the cantilever arms broke, killing many of the workers.

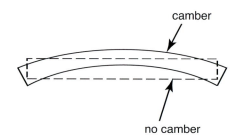

After reevaluation of the design, work recommenced in 1909, and the project successfully reached completion in 1917. The bridge was designed to accommodate a train, three lanes of auto traffic, pedestrians, and even a streetcar.

The Lake Pontchartrain Causeway in Louisiana, a prestressed concrete bridge, has two separate parallel spans.

BEAM AND GIRDER BRIDGES

Girder, or beam, bridges can be quite elegant, because they typically involve the least amount of visible structure. Indeed, a simple log across a stream is also a beam bridge—a continuous member connecting two sides of a gap is all that is required for this type of bridge. Beam bridges can span a wide range of distances, depending on how many beams are connected together. For a single beam, as opposed to a series of linked beams, the maximum span is around 250 feet (76 meters).

Typically, beam bridges consist of a horizontal girder supported at each end. The girders can be made of a variety of materials. Two main types of girders are used in modern steel bridges. One is an I-beam, a type of girder consisting of a vertical piece called a web, and two horizontal members, called flanges, on either end. The I shape is structurally sound and uses a minimum of material. Another type of girder is a box girder, so named because it is shaped like a box with two flanges and two webs.

Prestressed concrete beams are another good choice for constructing beam bridges. (The formation of prestressed concrete is discussed in detail in Chapter 5.) These beams feature steel rods embedded into the concrete framework and then pulled, or tensioned. The ends of the steel rods are then fixed to the end of the concrete beam to create one concrete-and-steel packaged beam. Prestressing causes a slight bowing in the beam, which is offset by the later weight of the bridge's loads. Since concrete performs well when compressed, and steel can withstand tension, the pairing of concrete and steel is ideal for a bridge.

The Lake Pontchartrain Causeway in Louisiana is one of the world's longest bridges of any kind and is actually two continuous-span beam bridges that are linked together. At a length of approximately 24 miles (54 kilometers), the causeway consists of 2,243 interconnected spans on the south side and 1,500 spans on the north. It was built of prestressed concrete beams that were carried to the site on barges. The Lake Pontchartrain Causeway survived Hurricane Katrina in 2005 with minimal damage, and became an important route for rescue workers into the damaged city of New Orleans. Another notable girder bridge, which is one of the largest typical girder bridges, is the Ponte Costa e Silva in Rio de Janeiro, Brazil. This bridge has a total span of 2,100 feet (640 meters).

THEMES WITH VARIATIONS

Located in Quebec, Canada, the Champlain Bridge is an example of a cantilevered bridge.

There are many variations on these four bridge types. Cantilever bridges are one such variation. This structurally innovative solution can involve girders or truss systems. In a cantilever bridge, two large beams are anchored on each bank of the body of water to be spanned. These beams project, or cantilever, across the water and are connected by a third beam. Cantilever bridges typically span between 1,800 and 2,000 feet (548 and 609 meters). The structural framework for a cantilever bridge can be either a simple beam-girder design or a more complicated truss framework.

Cable-Stayed Bridges

Cable-stayed bridges are a special type of suspension bridge, and they are some of the most beautiful bridges ever created. They are structurally similar to suspension bridges, but with a key difference. Both types

Cable-stayed bridges are a particularly beautiful example of elegant bridge design. Pictured is the Vasco da Gama Bridge in Portugal.

have towers and both have roadways that hang from cables. The difference lies mainly in the type and number of cables. Suspension bridges tend to utilize two major cables with any number of smaller hanging cables to support the bridge deck. These major cables usually run through holes in the supporting towers and are not directly connected to them. Cable-stayed bridges, on the other hand, use a series of slanted cables to support the load, and these cables are directly connected to the supporting towers.

Many cable-stayed bridges are cantilevered, with the beams supporting more of the bridge weight near the ends and the cables supporting more of the weight toward the middle of the bridge. The cables have both diagonal and vertical forces exerted on them, which means the deck must be sturdier than in a traditional suspension bridge. On the positive side, smaller anchorages are generally used because there is less horizontal force for them to counter.

Cables can be attached to the tower in a number of different patterns, including radial and parallel. A radial pattern is one in which the cables radiate from one point on the tower and extend to different points along the roadway. In a parallel pattern, the cables are attached along the side of the tower at various points and run parallel to each other. Designers can take many liberties with cable-stayed bridges, creating unusual patterns with the cables. One example is the Sundial Bridge in Redding, California, completed in 2004. Designed by Santiago Calatrava, this freestanding bridge has only one large pylon. Its glass-and-granite deck is supported by about 4,300 feet (1,310 meters) of cable.

Typical cable-stayed bridges span between 360 and 1,540 feet (110 and 470 meters). One of the most exceptional cable-stayed bridges is the Tarata Bridge in Japan. This bridge crosses the Seto Inland Sea and has a total length of 4,855 feet (1,480 meters). In addition to cables, this bridge also makes use of box girders. It was originally planned as a suspension bridge, but engineers discovered that if they used a cable-stayed design, they could avoid larger anchorages that would have had a negative impact on the surrounding landscape.

Drawbridges

At the other end of the spectrum from modernistic cantilever bridges are drawbridges—an ancient bridge type with many modern applications. Present-day drawbridges have a deck that can either tilt or move completely out of the way to allow tall ships to pass. Without a drawbridge, these vessels would either crash into the bridge or be forced to take another route that allowed for their passage.

Drawbridges were typically used in medieval Europe. Castle residents often surrounded themselves with water-filled moats for protection. A drawbridge at the main entrance to the castle allowed the guards to deny passage to certain visitors.

Modern drawbridges, such as Chicago's Dearborn Street Bridge, allow tall ships to pass through metropolitan areas.

THE CASTLE GATE

Early drawbridges were usually made of wood. The simplest designs consisted of a plank spanning the water between a castle and the grounds beyond its moat. When an enemy approached, guards would pick up the plank and remove it, thereby foiling the enemy's attempt to enter the castle. Later drawbridges involved anchoring a massive door to the castle walls with a system of pulleys and ropes. When lowered, the door served as a passageway across the moat. When the door was raised, the only way to access the castle was to swim (at one's own risk!) through the moat.

3

THE CONSTRUCTION SITE

Before construction can begin on a bridge, a site must be selected. Determining the best location to cross a body of water has been important to human survival since early migratory civilizations traveled to follow the seasons and the animals they hunted. Prior to the advent of bridges, early humans found shallow places in streams or rivers where they could cross.

FORDS

Fords are shallow areas in rivers and streams that can be crossed on foot by people and animals. Fords often occur where a river is wide as well as shallow, and with a relatively slow current.

Fords are shallow places in a river where people and animals can cross by foot, such as on this river in Korea.

The physics of how water moves reveals why a wide, shallow place is a good river crossing for travelers on foot. Flow in a river is governed by the "continuity equation." This equation expresses the relationship between the shape of the river channel and the velocity at which the water flows. The continuity equation states:

$$Q = v \times w \times d$$

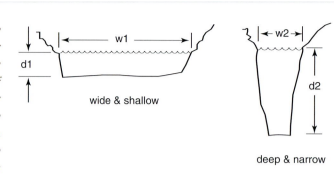

wide & shallow

deep & narrow

where Q is the discharge rate, v is the flow rate, w is the width of the river channel, and d is the depth of the river channel.

For a constant discharge rate Q, the continuity equation says that an increase in the width w will be accompanied by a decrease in the flow rate, or velocity, v. A decrease in the width w will be accompanied by an increase in the flow rate v. For a constant discharge rate Q and a constant velocity v, an increase in width means that the river depth d must decrease, and a decrease in width means that the river depth must increase. The continuity equation helps us understand why, in general, places on a single river are either wider and shallower with a slower velocity, or deeper and narrower with a faster velocity.

Wider portions of rivers tend to have slower flowing water because there is more space for the water to travel, when compared to a narrower portion of the river.

When looking for a good place to cross a river on foot, a place where the river is wide, shallow, and slow is definitely preferable to one where the river is narrow, deep, and fast. When fording a river on foot or horseback, the main considerations are that the water is shallow enough to walk through and the flow velocity is slow enough not to sweep a traveler off his or her feet. The continuity equation helps us understand how the same river can have places suitable for fords, and other places where the river is much faster and deeper. Of course, when building a bridge, the width that must be spanned (and thus the length of the bridge) can be more important than the velocity of the water beneath it.

TRANSPORTATION AND GEOGRAPHIC CONSIDERATIONS

While fords are good places to cross a river on foot, they are not necessarily good places to build bridges. Bridge builders have to consider a number of different factors when choosing an optimal location.

Travel routes are one of the first considerations in choosing a site for a bridge. A bridge is only worth building if it is useful. The historic Navajo Bridge in Glen Canyon National Recreation Area in northern Arizona is one of only seven crossings of the Colorado River for a stretch of 750 miles (1,207 kilometers). Before the bridge was built, travelers from Utah to Arizona had to make a detour of 800 miles (1,287 kilometers) around Glen Canyon in order to cross the river, or take a hazardous trip across the river on a ferry. The Navajo Bridge, completed in 1929, made travel significantly easier in this region. While the bridge only spans 800 feet (244 meters) across the canyon, it was difficult to construct because of the steep sides of the canyon and the remote location, which made transport of materials to the site problematic. At the time of its construction, Navajo Bridge was the highest steel-arch bridge in the world. It now serves as a pedestrian bridge, with a modern replacement nearby that can carry heavier loads.

Bridge designers also have to look at the preexisting infrastructure. Most bridges are built for cars, and therefore should connect to roads that already are in place. Locating a bridge far from current roads is not practical, even if such a location would be easier or less expensive in terms of construction.

The remote location of the Navajo Bridge, and the steep walls of the canyon it spans, made its construction very difficult.

SHIPS' PASSAGE

Many bridges span canals, rivers, bays, or other waterways. In areas where shipping is common, bridge designers must consider how vessels will pass under or through a bridge. Shipping traffic can also affect site selection. For example, large cargo ships require a minimum channel depth through which to travel. Most bridge designs have a high central section free of piers or other supports under which ships can pass, or a section that lifts or spins as a drawbridge. Bridge designers must ensure that the channel depth in the center of the main passage is sufficient to allow the largest ships, fully laden with cargo, to safely traverse the bridge. In some areas, where bridge design and construction alters the preexisting profile of the channel bottom, dredging may be required. This deepens the main shipping channel so that ships do not scrape the bottom. Any material dredged up must then be disposed of properly.

After choosing a general setting, engineers and bridge architects analyze the site to come up with the best location for the bridge. One of the first measurements considered is the final length of the span. The longer a bridge, the more expensive and difficult it will be to build. When building a bridge over a canyon, river, or other topographic obstacle, bridge designers look for the shortest possible crossing.

Designers and engineers must also consider what lies between the bridge's two endpoints. If the bridge is to span a shallow water channel, a simple bridge with multiple columns supporting it is the best design. However, if the channel is very deep, or if the bridge will have to cross a gorge or canyon, it may prove too difficult to place supporting vertical shafts under the central part of the bridge. In this situation, the two endpoints of the bridge will support most of the structure's weight, so their placement and the type of material in which they will be embedded becomes very important.

GEOLOGICAL ANALYSIS

The engineers and architects responsible for locating bridge sites must conduct a thorough geological analysis of the rocks and other materials that are found at the site. Geologists are usually consulted to create a detailed geologic map that shows the makeup of the terrain at a proposed site.

A bridge's foundation will be much sturdier if it is anchored to bedrock rather than loose, unconsolidated material. Geologists determine whether bedrock exists at or near a potential bridge endpoint, and they can also tell its age and condition. Very old rock that has weathered significantly over tens of thousands of years is much less stable than more recent rock deposits. Sedimentary rock, made up of multiple layers usually deposited in an aquatic environment, is less stable than igneous (volcanic) or metamorphic (heated or otherwise processed) rock.

Sedimentary rock is layered, and while it may be very sturdy vertically, it has built-in fault zones in the direction parallel to its deposition. If a force is applied in the direction of these zones, the rock may move or become deformed. Regardless of whether a force is applied gradually due to the weight of a fully loaded bridge or abruptly, as in the event of an earthquake, movement could disrupt the bridge's foundation. It is also important to try to match soil types on both sides of a bridge, so that in the event of an earthquake, both sides of the bridge will undergo the same physical response. A bridge that shakes

Because sedimentary rock is layered, it can resist forces in some directions better than others.

Igneous rock, or volcanic rock, forms directly from molten rock that comes from deep beneath the surface of the Earth.

Metamorphic rock is rock, such as this marble, that has been changed due to high temperatures or pressures.

evenly at both ends will likely move as a unit in an earthquake and survive relatively undamaged. However, if one end of the bridge is fixed while the other end shakes violently, the bridge will be subject to significant internal stresses and likely be damaged.

Consider the case of a bridge in Iceland that had each anchorage embedded in a different soil type. After suffering damage in an earthquake, the bridge was outfitted with instruments that measured its response to seismic activity. Engineers discovered that the two sides of the bridge had very different responses to the earthquake's shaking, and this differential put a substantial strain on the entire structure. A new bridge is currently being built downstream at a site where both ends can be anchored in bedrock. This will produce a solid foundation that will minimize impact from any future earthquakes and will ensure that any shaking that does occur will apply to the bridge as a whole.

BROOKLYN BRIDGE

In the late 1800s, the 1,595-foot (486-meter) span of the Brooklyn Bridge was a symbol of the major advances made in construction and engineering in the United States. It was, at the time, the world's longest suspension bridge. The story of the Brooklyn Bridge began in 1866, when New York State approved the construction of a bridge over the East River, connecting the boroughs of Brooklyn and Manhattan. John Augustus Roebling, the bridge's designer, submitted plans for the bridge the following year. Unfortunately, he was killed as the result of an accident in 1869. In a tragic series of events, a ferry knocked into the building materials Roebling was standing on, his foot was mangled, and he died of tetanus shortly thereafter. His son Washington Roebling took over as chief engineer.

By 1870, caisson construction on the Brooklyn side of the bridge had begun. Caissons are enormous hollow boxes that allowed workers to begin the underwater task of clearing the seafloor. Since they were made of wood, the caissons were prone to fires. In addition, increased pressure from working underwater caused a sickness known as the bends in many of the workers, leading to illness and death. Roebling himself succumbed to this decompression illness and was forced to work mostly from his home. His wife, Emily, supervised much of the construction in his place.

The Brooklyn Bridge stands as one of America's most iconic examples of a suspension bridge.

Construction of the Manhattan caisson began the following year. It was finished by 1875, by which time the towers on either side of the river had also been completed. Because the road deck had yet to be installed, temporary ropes were strung from tower to tower, allowing workers to travel back and forth. Moving across this temporary bridge still took at least twenty-five minutes, so a wooden footbridge was added to facilitate worker transport.

The cables were built in 1876. Smaller cables were rotated and twisted to form larger cables. Despite some technical problems and a lawsuit involving the cable provider, work continued and construction of the road deck began in 1878. The Brooklyn Bridge design incorporated open trusses that, fortunately, held up well to wind and other forces. Suspenders (additional tensile supports that worked alongside the vertical cables) were used when building the road. These were hung from the cables and attached to small portions of the deck as it progressed. This process went on for several years, and construction on the bridge finally reached completion in 1883. The approaches—the portions of road leading up to the actual bridge—had been designed to be fairly elaborate, but were toned down in later updates.

The Brooklyn Bridge opened up an entirely new world of possibility for New

Using steel and granite to span New York City's East River, the Brooklyn Bridge transports people and vehicles at a maximum height of 135 feet (41 meters) above the water.

York citizens, both in terms of the development of the transportation industry and in expanding New York City's work force. These engineering feats served as an example to future bridge designers. Today, the Brooklyn Bridge is one of America's most influential bridges, and an irreplaceable part of New York's skyline.

ON SACRED GROUND

In the United States, a site's cultural history must be researched before ground is broken for any type of major construction. Once a site has been selected, a study of the area is conducted, as set out in the National Historic Preservation Act of 1966. The study serves to ensure that either no cultural artifacts are present at the site or those that are present will not be disrupted by construction. However, even with this preconstruction inspection, artifacts are sometimes found after ground has been broken. During bridge replacement work on the Hood Canal Bridge in Washington State during 2004, construction was stopped soon after it began when workers found artifacts. They were later determined to have come from the ancestral burial ground of an ancient Native American village called Tse-whit-zen. The project was halted immediately and a new site was selected for the bridge, requiring the site-study process to begin all over again.

SURVEYING THE SITE

In conjunction with geologic mapping of the site, surveyors usually create topographic maps to produce a complete site survey. When building a bridge, it is important to survey the site to a high degree of accuracy, so that both sides of the bridge will eventually meet. To visualize this procedure, think of laying railroad tracks, starting at two towns, and hoping to meet in the middle. If the placement of the tracks is not completely accurate, they will not line up when they meet. If the two sides of a bridge are constructed and end up being off by a few feet, the bridge will be useless.

A topographic map shows an area as seen from above, with contour intervals indicating the height of features measured from an arbitrary starting point (usually sea level). To construct a topographic map, a surveying team begins with a known starting point. Such points used to be

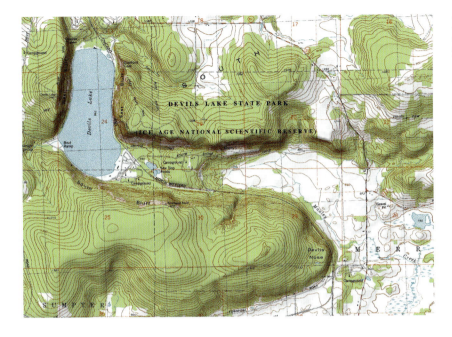

Topographic maps are useful for surveying a site, which is a routine part of bridge design.

physical benchmarks placed in the ground by previous surveying teams. Today, with the advent of handheld global positioning system (GPS) devices that give latitude, longitude, and altitude, surveying is a much easier project. Still, GPS units are limited to an accuracy of a few feet for civilian applications, though military GPS units are said to be much more accurate, so old fashioned surveying techniques are still necessary in many instances.

To survey a site, one member of a surveying team stands at a known benchmark holding a reflective pole marked with elevations. Such poles usually have a built-in level so that they can be held in a perfectly vertical position. Another member of the team stands at a position of unknown altitude. The exact distance and direction to the new point is measured using a compass and measuring wheel or a more high-tech equivalent. The team member at the new position uses a small telescope or a laser sensor to measure the elevation offset to the pole at the original point. The location and altitude of the new point are marked down on a grid, and then the process is repeated over and over again to find the relative location and elevation of many points in the mapping area.

Once a sufficient number of points is measured, a topographic map is constructed by hand, or the information can be entered into a computer program that builds the map. The exact elevations of the proposed endpoints are compared so that engineers can determine if the elevations are similar enough for bridge construction to proceed or if the area will have to be graded to produce elevations that are a better match. In extreme situations, the bridge endpoints are relocated to sites that are more compatible.

4

CALCULATING DESIGN LOADS

In addition to purely aesthetic considerations, bridge designers must also take into account how a bridge will support its live loads from traffic and wind, and its static loads from the weight of the bridge itself. Different types of bridges are subject to different forces and are appropriate for different situations. Materials are also chosen carefully, based on whether they can withstand the predicted forces.

FORCES

Bridge design must take into account all possible usage conditions—from a single car in the middle of the night to a fully loaded morning commute.

Bridge design is, quite literally, a balancing act. A bridge must be able to support various types of temporary and permanent loads, or pressures that act upon it. The worst possible result of a poor design is the collapse of a bridge that is unable to withstand a series of forces, perhaps leaving death and destruction in its wake. First, a bridge must be able to support its own weight, standing up to the force of gravity. Each of the major bridge types uses a different technique, depending on its method of construction, to support its static load.

All bridge architects and engineers must carefully consider the forces of tension and compression. Tension relates to the stretching or expanding of

BUILDING MATERIALS

Building materials for a bridge are chosen in part based on how they will respond to the various forces the finished bridge will have to bear. Different materials can have very different reactions to tension and compression. Think about a chain made of metal links. This chain is very strong under tension—even two strong people pulling on each end are unlikely to break it. However, under compression the chain crumples up and does not give any support at all. Some metal materials, like a steel beam, can be strong under both tension and compression. A cable, on the other hand, is very strong under tension but weak under compression because of its composition. Bridge designers also have to think about the forces that different parts of a bridge will have to withstand. For example, cables bear up to tension while the roadbed is compressed by traffic.

an object. Compression relates to the shortening or compressing of an object, resulting in its becoming smaller or denser.

To visualize these forces, consider a metal spring. When the two ends of the spring are pulled in opposite directions, the force of tension is applied, and the spring increases in length and becomes less closely packed. Pushing the ends of the spring together results in compression, and the spring decreases in length and becomes more closely packed.

Nature has a tendency to balance forces. If either tension or compression were the uncontested victor in the "Battle of the Bridge," the bridge would be rendered useless. Forces tend to either spread out, dissipate, or transfer, moving to areas that can better handle them. Keeping forces in balance is essential for a bridge to function.

Arch Bridges

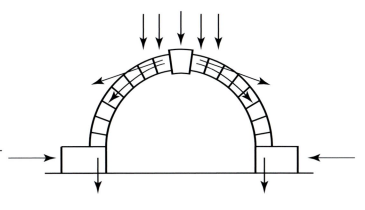

The arch bridges developed in ancient Rome are known for their elegant design. The arch is an interesting structural shape because it is almost exclusively under the force of compression.

To illustrate, if a thick piece of cardboard is bent into an arch shape and the ends are let go, they want to spring back to their original position. Arches are constantly exerting force away from the curve. In the case of a bridge, this force is directed toward the abutments, where the bridge meets the surrounding terrain. In a carefully designed arch bridge, there is little if any tension force because it almost completely dissipates. Stone is very strong under compression, and Roman arch bridges were usually built from stones carefully cut to shape. Some of these bridges were so strong that they are still standing today.

Beam Bridges

A typical beam under load experiences both compression (on the top surface of the beam, as the material is forced together) and tension (along the bottom surface, as the material spreads under load).

A beam bridge is essentially a horizontal beam—the deck—laid on top of piers at each end. Imagine a thin piece of wood supported by a brick at each end. If heavy rocks are placed at the center of the piece of wood, it would eventually start to bow and sag in the middle. This phenomenon is known as bending. When wood is bent in this way, a compression force pushes the wood fibers in the top of the board closer together. Force also affects the bottom of the board because as the top compresses, the bottom has no choice but to spread out. The tension force

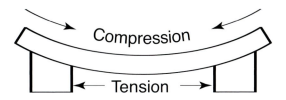

is responsible for this stretching action. A beam-bridge deck behaves in much the same way. Heavy loads cause the top surface of the deck to experience compression, while the bottom surface experiences tension.

Beam decks are designed with cross-sections that limit and control these forces. A cross-section is a vertical slice through a horizontal object, such as a beam or deck, that captures the shape of the object parallel to the ends. The larger the deck's cross-section, the more force it can dissipate. However, the interplay of forces is one reason that beam bridges can only span up to about 600 feet (182 meters). In the example of the piece of wood supported on bricks, a short piece of wood could support many rocks, but a much longer piece of wood would start to sag as soon as weight is piled on top of it.

Truss Bridges

Another clear example of a tension-and-compression system is the truss bridge, or a bridge with a structural system designed around one or more large trusses. Trusses use straight beam segments placed either vertically, horizontally, or diagonally to create triangles, which provide very stable support. A series of triangles forms a truss that is long enough to span the area to be crossed. Trusses can be placed either above the bridge deck, in a configuration called a through truss when above, or a deck truss when below. At each end connection is a pin, or hinged joint, which rotates, allowing it to move rather than twist. This is beneficial because torsion, or twisting, can cause a truss to collapse.

A truss bridge carefully balances the tension force, carried largely in vertical members, and the compression force, carried by horizontal and diagonal members.

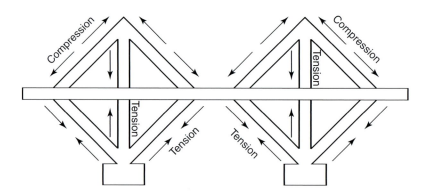

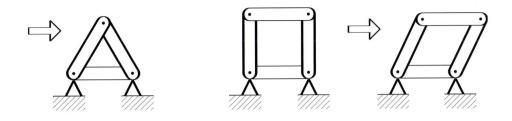

Triangular forms are very stable and not subject to bending in the presence of a horizontal force. In contrast, a hinged square form is extremely unstable when it comes to horizontal forces.

The vertical beams of a truss bridge are in tension, similar to the piers in a suspension bridge. The highest horizontal beams, as well as the diagonal beams, are in compression. The lowest horizontal beams are in tension, as well as shear and bending where necessary. Shear force, also called shear stress, is the force created by objects that lie parallel to each other, but attempt to move in opposite directions. It is also called the "sliding force," since it comes into play when objects in the same plane are pushed in different directions. Bending forces are created when the weight of Object A bears down on Object B so as to bend Object B out of position. One of the most structurally appealing aspects of a truss bridge is that, typically, forces such as bending and shear are almost nonexistent.

Trusses can be built in many configurations, each type offering a certain structural potential and design aesthetic. Some may be more elegant, but others may allow for longer spans. (See Chapter 2 for more information on truss patterns.) One thing that all successful trusses provide is stability. A stable configuration is one that will not collapse under pressure. A triangular shape is very stable. Pushing against the top or sides will not cause a triangular structure to fall. A square shape, on the other hand, is unstable because pushing horizontally on any of its sides will cause the structure to bend and collapse.

Suspension and Cable-Stayed Bridges

Suspension and cable-stayed bridges are structurally complex. Towers are usually built first, and then very large cables are raised into place near the tops of the towers. The decking is actually hung from these cables. Depending on the design, the bridge is either a suspension or cable-stayed type.

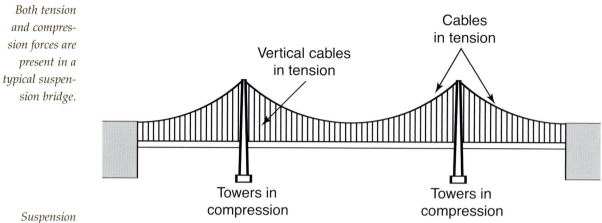

Cables
in tension

Vertical cables
in tension

Towers in
compression

Towers in
compression

Tension and compression are both major players in suspension bridges. The tension force is evident in the vertical cables that are supporting the deck, as they stretch and expand under the deck's weight. The deck is under a compression force from its own weight, as well as the various loads placed on it. This type of bridge is a perfect example of transferring forces, since the cables transfer their forces into the towers.

Supporting the Load

Bridges are under an enormous amount of pressure. There are two main categories of forces, or loads, that a bridge must support—temporary and permanent. Each type affects a bridge in a different way.

Temporary loads are those that change over time and may or may not be present depending on conditions. The main type of temporary load is the live load of pedestrians, cars, trucks, and trains that cross a bridge daily. Engineers must design the bridge to withstand the maximum reasonable load given the bridge's specific span. They must also take into account the construction load, which is the additional sustained weight of heavy construction equipment carried while the bridge is being built.

Other types of temporary loads include forces of nature. Earthquakes, tornadoes, and wind, in particular, contribute temporary loads that must be accounted for in the bridge's design. There are also impact loads, the so-called freak incidents, in which large, heavy objects fall onto a bridge deck, such as in an ice storm or a plane crash. Permanent loads—also called static or dead loads—are the forces that are present regardless of traffic on the bridge. They include the weight of the deck, cables, surfacing, guardrails, and anything else that is a permanent part of the bridge.

Against the Wind

Bear in mind that "typical" live and dead loads—traffic and bridge weight—are usually vertical. Forces such as wind are unpredictable and are often both vertical and horizontal, as wind comes from many different directions.

When designing a bridge to withstand wind forces, there are two main types of loads to consider. Wind can provide a constant load, meaning it is a consistent horizontal force pushing against the bridge. Wind can also be a dynamic load, meaning it pushes against the bridge both vertically and horizontally and changes over time. Some of the worst bridge disasters in history were partly due to dynamic loads that caused the bridge deck to twist, turn, and eventually break.

Wind uplift acts vertically upward, underneath a bridge, and can have devastating effects. Shown here is the Interstate 90 Bridge in Mississippi after Hurricane Katrina in 2005.

Another force to contend with is wind uplift. Uplift is a force exerted vertically upward, usually as wind passes under the surface of a bridge. To counteract uplift, decks are sometimes stiffened with a truss or other mechanism.

Other Forces

Any number of other minor forces can undermine the stability of a bridge. Consider thermal changes. The weather changes from day to day, even in moderate climates such as that of northern California, home of the Golden Gate Bridge. Hot steel has a tendency to expand, so very warm days cause expansion in various parts of the bridge. Similarly, very cold weather causes contraction. Bridges typically use expansion joints that allow some flexibility to accommodate these unpredictable forces.

Other forces are the result of the passage of time. Creep, or the regular settlement of loose dirt and other earth materials, has a negative effect on bridges. To offset this force, some elements of the bridge may be pre-loaded, or prestressed, so that when settlement occurs, the bridge will "relax" into the proper position.

BRIDGE RESPONSE TO FORCES

All bridges undergo some amount of physical movement due to the forces that act upon them. The most common of these forces are bending, shear, and torsion. We have seen how bending works in the plank-and-brick example. When a piece of wood is placed on bricks and weighted in the center, it will eventually start to bend. The same thing happens with larger-scale bridges.

Shear stress is a state created by parallel planes sliding against each other. The actual shape of a cantilevered-bridge deck, for example, can be altered due to wind shear. This occurs when winds change direction or increase in speed, causing crosswinds with increased force.

Torsion is the stress placed on an object that has been twisted. This can affect a long suspension bridge when high winds are present. Arch bridges and trussed-beam bridges are fairly resistant to torsion.

Have you ever had music turned up so loud that you felt the floor-boards shaking? This was most likely due to the phenomenon of resonance, which happens when a vibration causes something else to vibrate in its natural period of vibration. All objects have a particular way in which they would prefer to vibrate if subjected to the appropriate external stresses. An object that moves up and down sporadically is vibrating with

The bending force, which has an effect on any horizontal member upon which a load is placed, can often be counteracted by camber.

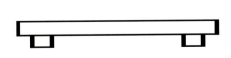

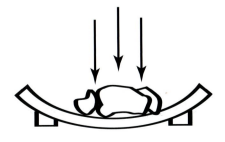

Bending

a particular period, or time between movements. If a force is applied at exactly the right points in the vibration cycle, the amplitude, or height, of the vibration can be increased dramatically. This is similar to leaning forward and backward at the right times while swinging on a swing. If the swinger leans forward and backward randomly, she will not go very high. However, if she leans forward while approaching the top of the swing's arc, and backward while moving in the other direction, she can increase

HANDLING STRESS

How are bridge stresses and forces addressed in actual bridge designs? One important requirement is flexibility. Bridges are designed to move up and down and side to side in response to changes in loads, temperature conditions, wind, and other factors. Deflections are measured from the natural position of the bridge, which usually comes from a straight line drawn between the two ends.

To further understand how deflections are designed into real bridges, consider San Francisco's Golden Gate Bridge. Here are some fast facts about the bridge. The total length is 1.7 miles (2.7 kilometers), or 8,981 feet (2,737 meters). The total length of the suspension span is 1.2 miles (1.9 kilometers), or 6,450 feet (1,965 meters). The bridge is 90 feet (27 meters) wide, and its average above-water clearance is 220 feet (67 meters). The total weight of the bridge, including approaches and anchorages, is 887,000 tons (805,000 metric tons). The maximum transverse (side-to-side) deflection in the center of the span is 27.7 feet (8.4 meters). The maximum downward deflection in the center of the span is 10.8 feet (3.3 meters), while the maximum upward deflection in the center of the span is 5.8 feet (1.7 meters). Think about that—the bridge is designed to flex up and down, without breaking, a total distance of more than 16 feet (4.8 meters)!

Shear is a force that tends to cause objects to slide apart or break along a plane.

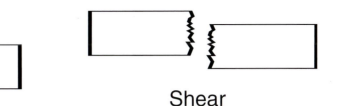

Shear

the height of the swing. The forces caused by leaning forward and backward are input at just the right times to fit with the natural rhythm, or period, of the swing.

Physical objects have a natural resonance, and bridges are no exception. One of history's most catastrophic bridge failures was that of Washington State's Tacoma Narrows Bridge four months after construction was completed in 1940. It was caused in part by the wind forcing the bridge to resonate at its natural period. As the wind applied forces to the bridge at just the right rhythm to match the bridge's natural period, the amplitude of the shaking of the bridge increased dramatically and contributed to the bridge's failure.

Axial forces are those that act along the longitudinal axis of a particular structural member. These forces are a major design consideration for cable-stayed bridges. Cables are the best choice for resisting axial forces, since they are vertically strong. Cables are very poor choices for compression forces, as previously mentioned.

BRIDGE CONSTRUCTION

Bridges are built in a specific sequence, generally based on structural and site considerations. Typically built first is the substructure of the bridge, which transfers the weight of the bridge into the ground. The substructure usually consists of vertical columns, or piers, and abutments, which are the structures connecting the end of the bridge to the ground. The superstructure is generally built next, and consists of the main deck of the bridge, which typically spans between the prebuilt piers.

TYPES OF SUBSTRUCTURE

Among the most fundamental aspects of a bridge substructure are the abutments. These structures, located at each end of the bridge, support the loads from the superstructure. They also serve to hold back any soil that may have been excavated while preparing the ground for the bridge foundation, and are the main connection between the bridge and the embankments at each end of the area spanned by the bridge.

Bridge construction is a dangerous endeavor, and is executed by skilled workers without a fear of heights.

In addition to abutments, most long-span bridges require piers that extend deep into the bedrock. Piers are structural columns that help

Abutments, such as these of the Brooklyn Bridge in New York, are a critical part of the bridge support system.

support the weight of the bridge's center span. Their design depends on the site conditions. Structural engineers must study wind forces, live and dead loads, depth of the water, and other factors before the piers can be designed and built.

Bridge piers require substantial footings, or connections to the ground beneath. In many cases, caissons are used. These are massive, inhabitable foundations sunk into the bedrock or the lowest point of the riverbed, depending on the anticipated depth of a bridge's foundations. Caissons usually contain an access channel and pressurized air system so that workers can actually descend (from the surface down into the caisson itself) in order to work on the bridge's foundation. Caissons come in several varieties, but are generally made of concrete. Once the workers' tasks are completed, the caissons are filled with a heavy material, such as concrete, and become a permanent part of the foundation structure. Piers are then constructed on top of the caissons.

One of the most hazardous aspects of working inside a caisson is the toll it takes on the human body. Workers have to descend through the depth of the water to get into the caisson, and similarly have to rise back up to the surface when the workday is over.

Caissons, such as these from the San Francisco Bay Bridge construction (1935), allow workers to complete the underwater portions of the bridge construction.

Ascending too fast or staying underwater too long allows excess nitrogen to build up in the human body. This causes a condition called the bends, or decompression sickness, a problem also encountered by divers when they rise to the surface too quickly. In the early days of bridge construction, workers would often become ill or perish while working in caissons. With appropriate precautions, though, this problem can largely be avoided.

Another important component of bridge substructure is the type of bearing used to transfer loads from the deck to the foundation and substructure. Bearings are assemblies that are used to reduce friction. One familiar example is a ball bearing, which uses round balls as rollers. Bridges use several types of bearings to help transmit loads. Some of the most common are roller bearings and sliding bearings.

TYPES OF SUPERSTRUCTURE

The superstructure is the part of the bridge that is most visible. It consists of the structure of the deck and the towers or cables supporting it. Bridge superstructures are typically made of steel, concrete, or timber.

Steel

Steel superstructures come in several forms. One of the most common types of steel deck is a steel beam or a beam with a cover plate. The addition of a cover plate, typically made of a reinforced polymer, adds extra stability (and, of course, cost) to the beam. A box-girder bridge has a deck section shaped like a box. This extremely stable bridge design is often used in short-span bridges. Box-girder bridges usually span no more than 350 feet (106 meters). Plate-girder bridges have a cross-section often shaped like a U, with the road deck occupying the bottom portion of the U shape. The two sides of the U are essentially I-beams, steel plates that have been welded together to form the structure of the deck.

Prestressed steel beams are another common type of bridge superstructure. Prestressed steel allows for a more flexible design because the steel sections are stressed to offset their own weight, making elaborate counter-weight devices unnecessary. Prestressed steel can also be used in arch bridges. Steel arches, which carry loads mainly through compression, are supplemented with prestressed arch ribs, usually plate girders or box girders. Concrete foundations then supplement the arch by transferring the loads from the ribs into the abutments on each side of the bridge.

The New York Queensboro Bridge is shown under construction here in 1907.

Concrete

Concrete superstructures are another popular choice for bridge design. Since concrete is strong in compression but weak in tension, it is reinforced with steel bars or cables. The steel gives the concrete strength to

UNDER PRESSURE

When a diver is underwater, the weight of the water exerts a pressure that pushes on the diver from all directions. The pressure exerted by the fluid is directly related to the weight of the water above the diver. For a static fluid, meaning one that is not moving, the pressure is equal to the weight of the water divided by the surface area:

$$Pressure = weight/area$$

The weight of an object is defined as mg, where m is the mass of the object and g is the acceleration of gravity. The symbol for area is A. The mass of an object is ρ (Greek letter rho), which is the density of the object, multiplied by V, which is the volume of the object:

$$Pressure = weight/area = \rho Vg/A$$

But the volume of an object is equal to the height times the area:

$$Pressure = weight/area = \rho Vg/A = \rho hAg/A = \rho gh\rho$$

This derivation shows that the pressure exerted on an object in a fluid is equal to ρgh, which is the density times the acceleration of gravity times the height. For a diver underwater, h is the depth beneath the surface. So, as a diver goes deeper and deeper underwater, the pressure increases.

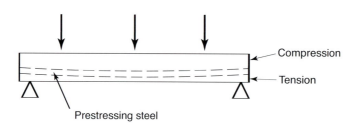

The top of a reinforced beam—under a load—is in compression, while the bottom portion of the beam is in tension. Concrete works well in compression, so the added steel helps resolve the tension force.

Compression

Tension

Prestressing steel

withstand tension forces. This material is called reinforced concrete, and almost all concrete used structurally is reinforced. To further increase its strength, the reinforced concrete is commonly prestressed when used in applications such as bridges.

Prestressed Concrete

Prestressed means that the concrete is loaded (either pretensioned or post-tensioned, depending on the design of the bridge) before it is put into its load-carrying role. Prestressed concrete can often carry heavier loads and be used for longer spans than regular reinforced concrete.

Prestressed concrete is made in two ways, using a mold. For pretensioned concrete, steel rods or wires are laid into the mold first. The rods are stretched, the concrete is poured and hardened, and then the rods are released. The concrete beam itself is then in compression because, over time, the steel rods will relax back into their prestretched shape. Pretensioned concrete beams are usually created off-site because the steel requires very strong anchors in order to stay stretched.

Bridge construction often involves barges or other vessels to help move large portions of the bridge into position. This technique was used in the Sydney Harbour Bridge in Australia.

Post-tensioned concrete, on the other hand, is made by placing unstretched steel rods into the mold. The rods are stretched after the con-

CURVED BRIDGES

The shortest distance between two points is a straight line. In spite of this, bridge spans often incorporate curves. Some bridges curve to take advantage of terrain or to find more favorable footings, others for aesthetic reasons. Is it harder to design a curved bridge than a straight one? Not necessarily, though there are extra considerations. For example, curved-steel deck girders are under more stress than straight girders. They are subject to additional torsion force, because cars that travel along these curved girders cause both a vertical downward force and a twisting force as they drive along the curve. This torsion causes additional shear stress in the beam, which could lead to failure if the beam is not appropriately designed. One design solution is to create a composite steel beam with a deeper cross-section, which helps resist the twisting force.

crete has been poured and hardened, usually by hydraulic machinery. Post-tensioning is best put to use in large sections of concrete where there can be expansion and contraction from weather and other forces; bridges are excellent uses for post-tensioned concrete.

Another important consideration when using concrete in bridge design is where the concrete will be poured. Precast concrete, whether it is reinforced with steel or not, is usually made in a factory by pouring the concrete in a reusable mold, then allowing the concrete to cure and harden before its transport to the construction site. In contrast, cast-in-place concrete is typically mixed off-site, then trucked to the construction location and poured right into place. Casting concrete in place allows for large, unique pieces that would be too large or unwieldy to transport.

Concrete Forms

Concrete deck beams, or girders, can come in all sorts of different configurations. The box girder is a common type. This beam is usually constructed as a hollow box, which is a very stable structural form. Concrete slabs can also be used as a deck. A concrete slab, usually made off-site, is a solid rectangular section often interwoven with steel cables or wires.

Concrete arches can also be used as a prominent element in bridge design. One of the more spectacular examples of this technology can be seen in the New Svinesund Bridge, a highway bridge between Norway and Sweden. It combines a steel superstructure with a concrete arch that serves as both super- and substructure. The arch, made of reinforced concrete, supports steel decking and actually rises about 100 feet (30 meters) above the top of the deck.

There is a wide range of concrete bridge types today. One elegant example is the Creve Coeur Lake Memorial Park Bridge in St. Louis, Missouri, which consists of a pair of bridges located four inches (20 centimeters) apart from each other. This bridge has cast-in-place concrete in its 2,675-foot (815-meter) spans, each of which is made of a hollow concrete box. The deck uses prestressed concrete in cantilever construction.

Another modern concrete bridge is the Fifth Street Bridge, over the Miami River in Dayton, Ohio. This minimalist bridge

The Arlington Memorial Bridge in Washington, DC, is an example of a masonry-arched bridge that combines grace, elegance, and a relatively minimalist visual support system.

uses prestressed concrete deck girders combined with exterior girders whose depth varies from narrow to wide, then back to narrow.

Timber

A third type of superstructure is timber, or wood. Remember the log placed across a stream? That was an example of the most basic type of wood bridge. Building on that basic concept, timber bridges become much more complicated when the spans and expected loads increase.

In parts of the world where lumber is a bountiful natural resource, timber bridges make economic sense and are used more often than in places where wood is scarce. Timber-beam bridges are fairly common in Australia, for example, and many use a simple beam and deck-plank design.

Many modern timber bridges use glue-laminated timber, commonly known as glulam. Several layers of wood beams are essentially glued together, under pressure, with a structurally sound adhesive. Each glulam beam is designed to carry a specific load. The lamination technique increases the amount of weight that a wood beam can support. This construction method has been used in bridges in the United States for about sixty years.

Composite timber bridges use different building materials to create a bridge with increased strength. A reinforced concrete deck, for example, might be combined with wood trusses or other elements. Although composite timber bridges may cost more than timber only bridges, they generally last much longer.

BRIDGE
SAFETY

The structural integrity of a bridge is clearly of chief importance. If not well designed, a bridge will fail and lives may be lost. A bridge must be safe enough that pedestrian, automotive, train, or other traffic can cross it without fear of injury. To ensure safety, bridges employ several designed elements—guardrails, traffic barriers, walkways, and lighting—all of which help to keep bridge travelers headed down the right path.

GUARDRAILS AND OTHER SAFETY FEATURES

Guardrails are a necessary safety precaution and are used in virtually all bridges that support automobile traffic, such as the Brooklyn Bridge in New York.

One of the first lines of protection a bridge can offer automobiles is a guardrail. Also referred to as approach rails, they can be made of different materials such as wood, metal, or concrete. They usually lead up to the bridge span, and their job is to ensure that traffic finds its way safely onto the bridge and not into the water. Approach rails continue across the span, at which point they are generally called bridge rails. Though standard on high-volume bridges, approach rails are not always used on bridges that carry fewer than 400 or 500 cars per day.

COVERED BRIDGES OF PENNSYLVANIA

Covered bridges are found in the midwestern and eastern United States and parts of Canada. These small bridges, built in the mid-nineteenth century, span approximately 100 to 120 feet (30 to 36 meters) and are usually made of wood. The reasons for covering these bridges are subject to debate. It may have been to provide shelter in foul weather, to help convince skittish animals to cross the river, or to protect the wooden trusses from snow, rain, and other weather. Extensive documentation does not exist for most covered bridges, so this section discusses how a generic covered bridge might have been built.

As with any major bridge project, covered wooden bridges most likely started with excavation at each end of the proposed span. Wooden planks were likely hewn off-site. There were probably floor joists running the direction of the span, with wood decking planks placed perpendicularly across them. More wooden members would have been secured to the undersides of the deck as cross braces. A single plate likely secured the deck to the riverbank, with additional boards or trusses serving to further stabilize the deck.

Wooden pegs probably held the various members together, so holes would have been drilled into the pieces so that they could be assembled on-site.

If the span was long enough, piers would support the middle of the bridge span. Abutments constructed at either end would have supported the bridge and, in some cases, kept the surrounding earth from falling into the water. Once the deck was constructed, the sidewalls were most likely built in place using wood slats arranged to form a lattice. Weatherboards would have been pegged to the outside of the lattice to provide a sheltered space inside. Chin braces—wooden posts that supported the top of the wall—would have been placed slanting toward the road deck.

Trusses supporting the roof were most likely built flat on the ground, then raised into place. Roof rafters would have spanned the trusses. Early covered bridges may have used shingle roofs, while later roofs were made of metal. Additional bracing would have been installed if the bridge was subject to high winds or other conditions. Many of these picturesque bridges still exist in rural areas.

Covered bridges were generally built on a small scale, unlike more modern and massive suspension bridges.

The Indian Timothy Memorial Bridge in Washington State adds safety via a simple array of vertical elements that support an arch.

One method of construction for guardrails involves steel angles, or pieces of steel with an L-shaped cross-section. Standard steel forms such as channels (having a C-shaped cross-section) are placed at intervals, and then are connected by side and top rails. Guardrails are often designed to be aesthetically consistent with the bridge.

While guardrails are often built on-site, they can also be prefabricated in a factory. For bridges with smaller spans, the end sections of the bridge may be cast with the guardrails already built in, and then trucked to the site for installation. This method provides a clean look, as well as easier on-site construction. The connection between a guardrail and a bridge rail is exceedingly important, as a poorly designed connection can lead to cars crashing into the gap between where the guardrail ends and the bridge rail begins.

Rails are not always strictly utilitarian. The design of a bridge rail can be an opportunity for the architect's vision to be seen down to the last detail. They can contain curves and openings that mimic those of the main bridge design. One example is the Indian Timothy Memorial Bridge in Washington State. Built in 1923 but no longer in use, this simple arched

DECKING

Regardless of a bridge's substructure and superstructure, all bridges must have some sort of decking. Without a deck surface, automotive and pedestrian traffic would not be able to traverse the bridge. While many bridge decks consist of concrete or steel, there are other options.

Composite decking can be created from a number of materials, including fiberglass and various polymers. These are usually easy to handle on-site and have a fairly quick installation time. Corrugated steel decking is another popular choice for its ease of installation; it is typically attached to concrete beams to form a sturdy, lightweight deck.

A road surface is placed on top of the deck structure. One of the most common surfacing materials is asphalt. This sticky black liquid is a petroleum derivative that dries quickly once cooled. Asphalt is used on bridges, roads, and parking lots because of its durability.

Another type of surfacing is latex concrete, which is concrete (sand, cement, and aggregate rock) mixed with latex and water. Once the deck surface is cleaned, latex concrete is poured to make a surface that is both durable and smooth, and often lasts longer than an asphalt surface.

bridge uses a mini-colonnade of railings to provide a counterpoint to the large superstructure. The arch detail in between the railings mimics the arch structure of the overall bridge.

When engineers bring their bridge designs to a municipality for final approval, the topic of guardrails often comes up because safety must be their primary function. While all bridge designers are aware of this, it is often tempting to design an elaborate railing that may not have the same safety value as something simpler and sturdier. This debate over aesthetics versus safety is one of many that arise over the course of designing and building a bridge.

Traffic Barriers

Another important safety consideration that goes into bridge design is that of median and traffic barriers. Median barriers are obstructions that help separate traffic that flows in opposite directions. Traffic barriers are usually positioned to help separate pedestrian and road traffic. Both types of barriers are necessary for bridges that experience heavy automotive traffic on a daily basis.

Traffic barriers come in several types. While they can be permanent, more often they are temporary, movable objects that can be repositioned as needed. For example, portable concrete traffic barriers can be hauled into place when one lane of a bridge must be closed. They can also be placed as needed for ongoing construction or other projects that require the diversion of traffic.

Traffic barriers can also be realigned to manipulate the flow of traffic on bridges used by commuters. For example, a bridge may have three of four lanes open for morning northbound traffic, but only two lanes northbound in the evening. In this case, movable barriers are erected and dismantled on a regular basis, perhaps even automatically.

Traffic barriers are often relocated at various times of day to accommodate different traffic loads, as seen here on the San Francisco Golden Gate Bridge.

Pedestrian Walkways

While carrying automobile traffic is the main purpose of most bridges, pedestrians also need a way to cross. Some people enjoy walking across bridges rather than driving in order to experience a bridge's true beauty, and some residents of metropolitan areas such as New York City may well commute by foot or bicycle. Protected pedestrian walkways are a necessity in the design of a safe, habitable bridge.

The key design element in a bridge walkway is its distance from the roadbed. Walkways must be either structurally isolated from the road, if they are to exist at the same level, or elevated above the bridge deck.

The pedestrian walkway to the Sydney Harbour Bridge in Australia uses a mixture of materials to create a certain atmosphere. The bridge is one of the world's longest arched steel bridges, and the steel patterns around the walkway reflect this design. The platform's lighter material

Pedestrian walkways, such as those on the Brooklyn Bridge, allow for foot traffic while also providing a community destination and tourist attraction.

This pedestrian walkway on the Sydney Harbour Bridge combines steel and concrete to create a distinct aesthetic, while also serving its function.

works well with the major concrete and granite pylons on either side of the bridge.

One particularly beautiful example of an elevated bridge walkway is the work of engineer Santiago Calatrava. The Alamillo Bridge in Seville, Spain, is a gorgeous cable-span bridge that uses a single asymmetrical pylon. The cantilevered roadway projects from the main beam, and the pedestrian walkway is raised above the level of the deck. Observers have a supreme view of the water, bridge, and surrounding city.

SIGNAGE AND LIGHTING

Very few people who use bridges ever give a thought to signage and lighting. Who cares where the lights go or how many warning signs there are? In fact, a bridge would not be passable at night or early in the morning without appropriate lighting. Without signs, drivers could get hopelessly confused about which lanes were open at what times, and this could easily cause accidents getting on and off the bridge.

PEDESTRIAN WALKWAYS

Pedestrian walkways are a required safety measure for any bridge that allows pedestrian traffic, but they need not be completely utilitarian. They can also be things of beauty. For example, the Brooklyn Bridge has a wooden walkway that is also a major tourist attraction. Wood slats provide a natural feel, while the steel rails and balusters add structural and safety components. People walking along the bridge have access to views that would be impossible to experience from a car.

Lighting

Aside from the obvious goal of making a bridge safe for nighttime use, bridge lighting has an aesthetic component. Lighting can be used to showcase the bridge's more interesting features and can make it appear as a true landmark when seen from a distance. The color of the lights used is also an issue; orange lighting, for example, may be more appropriate at dawn than bright yellow lighting. To ensure that the lights are in good working order at all times, lighting designers pay careful attention to wind, rain, and other conditions that might affect the lifetime of the lights.

Another consideration is what is known as light pollution. While drivers need to see at night, excess lighting can be both a waste of power and a nuisance. A city should not squander its resources on lighting up the night sky when it could spend less energy by focusing lights only on the areas where they are needed. One good solution is to design lights to point only downward, and use lenses or shades to keep the light focused on the part of the bridge requiring illumination. As little light as possible should be shining into empty space. Local residents, including amateur astronomers, appreciate restraint in this area.

Different types and intensities of lights are required at different parts of a bridge. The Golden Gate Bridge, for example, uses high-pressure sodium lamps for the roadway, but lower-intensity lights at the tops of the towers. The sidewalk lamps are low-pressure sodium, while each cable of the bridge is illuminated with 116-watt bulbs.

A variety of lights and fixtures are used in the construction of large bridges. The types just mentioned are some of the most common: roadway lights, tower sidewalk lights, tower lights, and cable lights. Pier navigation lights, midspan lights, and purely decorative lighting might also be placed at any point along the bridge or railings. Many of these lights adhere to design and Coast Guard standards. Pier navigation lights, for example, are usually red, while green lights are used to mark the center of a fixed bridge to aid in the smooth flow of boat traffic passing under the bridge.

Physics plays a large role in bridge lighting design as well. In some cases, particularly in cable-stayed bridges, there may be very little surface

Bridge lighting on the Golden Gate Bridge allows the bridge to be used at all times of day and night, while also creating a particularly beautiful scene.

The San Francisco–Oakland Bay Bridge uses careful lighting design that promotes visibility, while establishing this bridge as a California icon.

to reflect light. Reflectance is essential to the spreading of light, which makes the structure visible in darkness. To combat the problem with cable-stayed bridges, some designers use blinking metal halide lights that always appear in motion.

Reflective Signs

Traffic signs on bridges, like any road signs, must be visible to drivers at night as well as during the day. Signs can be illuminated in two ways: active illumination, in which lights are positioned to shine onto the signs, and passive illumination, which utilizes reflective paint. The difference in the two methods is the source of the light. With active illumination, the sign is lit continuously from dusk to dawn with specially placed lights. With passive illumination, a special reflective coating covers either just the lettering on the sign or the whole sign. This paint has small chips of

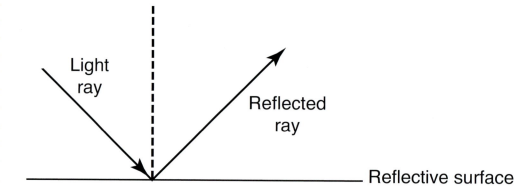

Light ray

Reflected ray

Reflective surface

reflective material in it that act like mirrors. When the light from a car's headlights hits the sign, a large portion of that light is scattered and reflected back at the car. This allows the driver to see the sign clearly, even if there are no streetlights.

While light from a car's headlights will reflect back from nonreflective signs and from other objects like fences and buildings, reflective coatings direct and focus the light from a car so that more of it returns, allowing the driver to see the sign with less of the light scattered off and lost in directions that are not useful. By carefully angling and aligning the reflective materials in the coating, engineers are able to greatly increase the amount of light reflected back to the viewer. This technique results in the letters or other reflective portions of the sign appearing much brighter than they would if they were painted with regular, nonreflective paint.

Signage

Signage is an important part of how a bridge is actually used. Well-placed, lighted signs inform those who use a bridge of the presence of high winds, the potential for an icy road deck, or other hazards. Signs are also used to inform drivers of specific travel information such as carpool hours, toll rules, and upcoming highway exits.

Modern electric signs are also helpful. Drivers are alerted to which toll lanes accept cash and which lanes may have the shortest drive-

Without bridge signage to direct people to use the right lanes at the right time, bridge traffic would be out of control and accidents would abound.

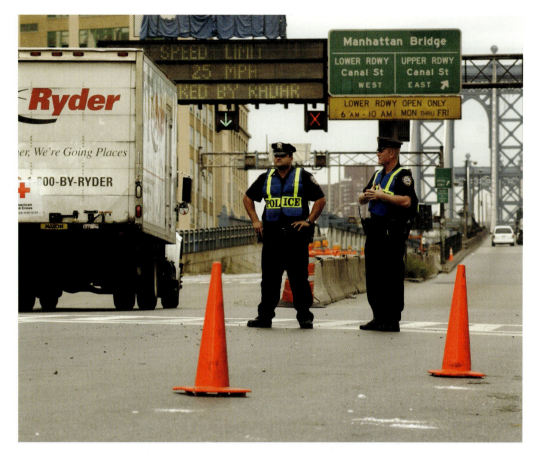

through time. The same signs can also indicate police activity, such as the presence of an Amber alert or a stolen vehicle emergency. The more a bridge designer plans for such signage, the less obtrusive it will be so the final bridge is a harmonious combination of structure, elegance, and safety.

UNUSUAL BRIDGES

Most traditional bridges are anchored at either side of the body of water or valley that they span; however, this is not always the case. Some bridges are designed to float on the surface of the water. Others are not permanently installed and are taken down once they are no longer required. Military bridges, for example, are often packed up or destroyed once troops have crossed them so that no one else can follow their route.

PONTOON BRIDGES

This pontoon bridge in India shows how a little creativity can create an entirely usable bridge structure out of unlikely materials.

The majority of bridges are permanent structures, fixed to the landscape by foundations and anchorages. However, for smaller, usually temporary crossings, it is possible to erect a pontoon bridge, or a bridge with floating supports. Used for thousands of years, pontoon bridges are a reliable way to quickly create temporary bridges using existing materials.

A pontoon is a floating, buoyant object whose sole purpose is to support weight. This weight can be either above or below the surface of the water. Buoyancy is an upward force exerted on any object immersed in a

BUOYANCY

Why do some objects sink when placed in water, while others do not? It all depends on the relationship between the weight of the object and the weight of the water it displaces. If an object weighs more than the water it displaces, then the force of buoyancy supporting it in water does not balance the force of gravity pulling down on the object. In this case, the object will sink. Small dense objects, like pebbles, sink, because they also do not displace enough water to compensate for their weight. Larger hollow objects, like huge cruise ships, float, because the weight of the water they displace is equal to the object's weight.

When something small and heavy is dropped into a tub filled with water, it will sink. When a large plastic toy boat is placed into the same tub, it will float. The behavior of these two objects is governed by how the density of the object, or its mass-to-volume ratio, compares with the density of water. Some fish can actually change their density at will to rise to the surface of the ocean or sink to the bottom. They accomplish this feat by increasing their volume while keeping their mass constant. To do this, they inflate a swim bladder, which is an inflatable pouch much like a lung, increasing their volume while leaving their mass unchanged. This process reduces their density to below that of water, allowing the fish to rise.

fluid, such as water. It is determined by Archimedes' Principle, named for the Greek physicist who discovered it, which states that the buoyancy force exerted on an object floating in liquid equals the weight of the fluid displaced by that object.

Pontoons can support temporary or permanent floating bridges, docks, or even occupied vessels such as houseboats. They are also commonly used as floats for seaplanes, allowing them to land on water. Some simple pontoons are simply overturned boats, while others are sealed, air-filled

Militaries often create pontoon bridges because they are fast to assemble and disassemble, and are easily floated down-river in their individual components.

vessels constructed specifically as supports. The simplest method of constructing a pontoon bridge is to connect a series of overturned boats. They are attached together in a stable fashion, and a deck, typically wood slats, is fixed to the boat bottoms.

PERMANENT FLOATING BRIDGES

While most pontoon bridges are temporary, a few floating bridges have been designed to last. One of the most impressive permanent floating pontoon bridges is the Evergreen Point Floating Bridge in Seattle. Built between 1960 and 1963, it is the longest floating bridge in the world, spanning 7,578 feet (2,309 meters). The bridge crosses Lake Washington between Medina and Seattle, and is used primarily by commuters. Unfortunately, due to the rapid population growth in this region, bridge use is far beyond capacity, causing frequent traffic jams and other holdups during peak commuting hours.

The Evergreen Point Floating Bridge is also a drawbridge with a middle span that retracts to allow tall vessels to pass through. When the draw-bridge is activated, the pontoons in the middle of the section simply roll underneath.

Why did the designers choose to build a pontoon bridge rather than a more traditional suspension bridge? Essentially, the length of the span,

Buoyancy can be shown in a simple experiment. An upward force is exerted by water onto objects immersed in it, and so a hanging weight appears to weigh less when submerged in water.

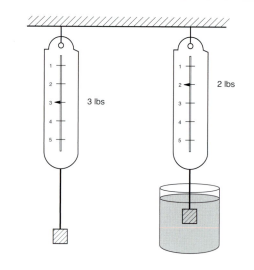

1.4 miles (2.2 kilometers) was too long and the lake too deep for a traditional bridge. The structure of the bridge consists of thirty-three full-sized pontoons made of prestressed concrete. Each one measures 360 by 60 by 14.8 feet (110 by 18 by 4.5 meters). The pontoons are stabilized by massive cables connecting them together in a chain.

Unfortunately, experts believe that the Evergreen Point Floating Bridge will have to be demolished once a replacement is built, because of its vulnerability to earthquakes. While there have been efforts to stabilize it for better seismic handling, the bridge now sits a foot lower in the water than it once did because of these extra weights and measures. In addition, an engineering study found that the supporting columns under the bridge's west end are starting to decompose. The bridge is typically closed in high winds, and any bridge with the amount of commuter traffic carried by Evergreen Point must be operational year-round. A replacement project is currently in development.

The second-longest floating bridge in the world is right next door to Evergreen Point. The Lake Washington Bridge (renamed the Lacey Murrow

The Evergreen Point Floating Bridge in Seattle, Washington, is the world's longest floating bridge.

Memorial Bridge) was built before Evergreen Point in 1940. It spans 6,620 feet (2,017 meters), and, like Evergreen Point, it crosses Lake Washington in Washington State. Designed by Homer Hadley, the bridge was intended to make it easier to travel between mainland Washington and Mercer Island. Like Evergreen Point, the Lacey Murrow Memorial Bridge was constructed using concrete pontoons, with a drawspan in the middle. Another similarity was the amount of traffic the bridge attracted; the number of vehicles passing over the bridge every day far exceeded the design loads. The Homer M. Hadley Memorial Bridge was built running parallel to this bridge in 1989 to alleviate the congestion.

Another floating bridge is the Okanagan Lake Bridge in British Columbia, Canada. The bridge spans 4,620 feet (1,408 meters), with the pontoon portion covering about 2,100 feet (640 meters). The central pontoons measure about 200 feet (60 meters) long and are connected with shorter pontoons at either end. The pontoons are cabled together to work as a single unit and submerged to a depth of about 8 feet (2.4 meters), though the depth varies somewhat due to weather and other conditions. The pontoons are anchored with weights totaling 140 tons (127 metric tons) that extend into the subsoil of the lake.

In keeping with what has become something of a common theme with pontoon bridges, the Okanagan Lake Bridge is also nearing the end of its useful life because traffic volume far exceeds its design loads. A larger replacement bridge is currently under construction. In a bit of bridge trivia, there is a local myth that Okanagan Lake is inhabited by a lake monster known as Ogopogo. This monster has changed over time from a lake devil to a green serpentine sea creature occasionally witnessed by locals and tourists.

Disasters Associated with Floating Bridges

The most obvious problem associated with a floating bridge is the possibility of sinking. One unfortunate incident began when the Lacey Murrow Memorial Bridge required some deck resurfacing and widening in 1990. Jackhammers were considered too slow, so engineers decided to use a high-pressure water system to blast off the excess

HOOD CANAL

Believe it or not, the Murrow Bridge was not the only bridge in the state of Washington to experience a sinking disaster. In a somewhat similar mishap, the Hood Canal Bridge, which spans the waters between the Olympic and Kitsap peninsulas, had a sinking problem of its own. This bridge was completed and opened for traffic in 1961. In 1979, high winds caused excessive pressure on the pontoons, which likely made the hatch doors burst open and allowed the pontoons to fill with water and eventually sink. The affected portion of the bridge was replaced and reopened by 1982.

material. For environmental reasons, this water could not simply be pushed into Lake Washington. It was decided to use space inside the pontoons to store the debris water, so the sealed doors to some of the pontoons were opened.

Unfortunately, the Seattle area experienced a large storm around this time. Because the doors in the pontoons had been left open, they filled up beyond capacity. Workers attempted to pump the pontoons dry, but it was a losing battle. A single pontoon eventually filled completely and sank. Since the pontoons were daisy-chained together by high-strength cables anchored to the lake floor, this pontoon dragged the others down with it. Piece by piece, the middle of the bridge slowly sank. Local television stations documented the sinking process. The Hadley Bridge then had to absorb extra traffic until the Murrow Bridge was replaced in 1994.

OVABLE BRIDGES

The most common use for movable bridges is in military maneuvers. These bridges are quickly built on-site of materials that are readily available or that soldiers have brought along with them. After a crossing, these bridges are either dismantled and packed up immediately, or destroyed to keep the enemy from using them.

One of the earliest designs for a movable bridge came from Leonardo da Vinci. A designer, artist, engineer, architect, and all-around Renaissance man, da Vinci designed many of the world's "firsts." He sketched the first bicycle, the first armored tank, the first airplane, and the first portable bridge. In the Codex Atlanticus, one of several compilations of his notebooks, a sketch and notes dating to around 1482 describe how to quickly gather tree trunks, tie them together with ropes, and secure them in order to create a fast temporary crossing.

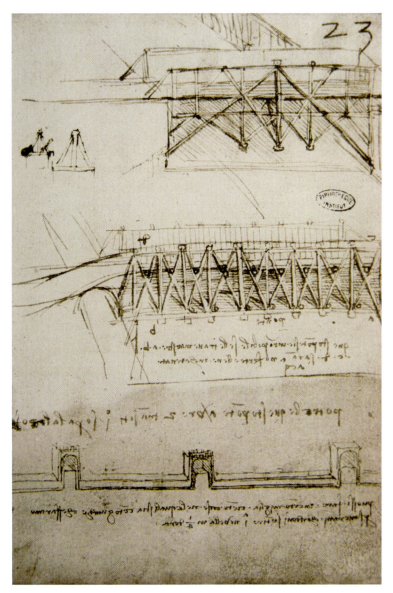

One of the most common early military bridges was a type of pontoon bridge. The pontoons were usually boats connected by rope, with barrels sometimes placed in between the pontoons to fill the

Leonardo da Vinci was designing portable military bridges as early as the fifteenth century.

TURTLE BAY SUNDIAL BRIDGE

Santiago Calatrava is an award-winning Spanish engineer and architect who has designed some of the most visually stimulating structures of the twentieth and twenty-first centuries. He has successfully completed many projects, including airports, stadiums, and bridges. His bridges are structurally innovative, and his engineering background enables him to create unusually artistic works that take full advantage of new construction technology. While most of his work is located in Europe, one of his recent bridge projects is in rural Redding, California—the Turtle Bay Sundial Bridge.

This steel-and-glass footbridge, which crosses the Sacramento River, truly stands out from the surrounding landscape. It is located between a science museum and an arboretum, and is surrounded by river trails.

The Turtle Bay Sundial Bridge is one of the world's most elegantly designed footbridges.

This was Calatrava's first project in the United States. It began in 1995, when the private McConnell Foundation solicited a design from Calatrava. Among other design requirements, the bridge could not sink concrete piers into the river below, since it was home to spawning salmon, so a suspension bridge was the best choice.

The design was finalized in 1997. The steel span has a glass deck anchored by a massive pylon that is tilted at a 42-degree angle; the upward pull from the cables then supports the decking. Walkways around the bridge were created of rammed earth, a method of construction whereby soil is mixed with various stabilizers and physically compacted into a solid form. While detractors thought a simpler concrete bridge would have suited the area better, Calatrava persisted with his choice of materials and aesthetics.

Construction on the bridge got under way in late 2001. It was a fairly complex endeavor, since the entire structure consists of curving lines. The signature pylon, which provides the main aesthetic force behind the bridge, has a slight twist that required customized building procedures. The steel had to be tweaked and trimmed constantly so that the curved pieces fit together properly.

The steel deck consists of a giant truss, which was delivered to the site in pieces. After assembly, it was post-tensioned by

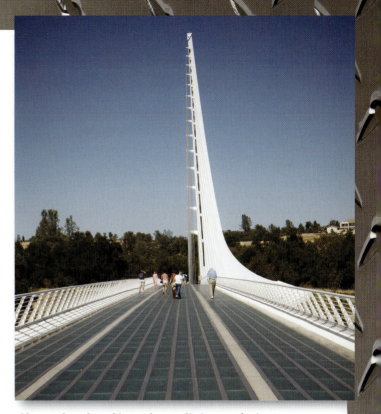

Glass and steel combine to form a distinct aesthetic.

more than 4,300 feet (1,310 meters) of suspension cables. More than 200 translucent glass panels were then laid in place for the decking and combined with veined granite for a surface that looked both high-tech and naturalistic. The deck was completed after the top of the 217-foot (66-meter) pylon, which resembles a sundial, was set into place. More than 580 tons (526 metric tons) of steel went into the pylon.

The bridge opened for foot traffic in 2004. Though the modern look and feel of the bridge deviates somewhat from the surroundings, Sundial Bridge is a work of art and an attraction in its own right.

gaps. More recently, plastic floats have been used to help maintain buoyancy. Whatever decking material was on hand would have been laid out, making the temporary bridge immediately serviceable.

While most military pontoon bridges span relatively short lengths, the longest on record spanned more than 2,000 feet (600 meters)! It was located

Pontoon bridges are used by modern militaries, as seen in this Vietnamese example.

The Bailey Bridge is a collapsible bridge system, which can travel with militaries. Some can be constructed in several days and can withstand substantial loads.

between Bosnia and Croatia along the Sava River and was in existence between 1995 and 1996.

For cases where large bridges are required for vehicles and equipment, military bridges today may come in collapsible kits. One of the larger-scale military bridge systems is the Bailey Bridge, which uses interlocking steel components to create a bridge of a predetermined size and an expanse of up to about 200 feet (60 meters). Bailey Bridges use cantilever construction to allow for fast installation without the aid of heavy formwork. However, these types of bridges cannot be assembled in a matter of minutes; most take days and require at least a small crew.

Some of the more modern military bridges come disguised as armored vehicles. Wheeled vehicles, such as armored tanks, come equipped with steel planks that can unfold to form a very quick (and highly portable) bridge. The spans are relatively short, usually less than 100 feet (30 meters), but the convenience factor alone is quite amazing.

BRIDGE

DISASTERS

All of the individuals involved in the creation of bridges—designers, engineers, construction workers—and those who use them, either as part of a daily commute or just occasionally, hope that bridges will remain safe, stable, and sound. Unfortunately, history has taught us that such security cannot be taken for granted. Countless minor bridge mishaps have occurred throughout history, and there have been a handful of spectacular bridge failures. In the wake of these catastrophes, engineers have studied the causes and gained a better understanding of how to create safer, more reliable bridges.

TACOMA NARROWS BRIDGE

Bridges can fail in a spectacular manner, as seen in the Minneapolis Freeway Bridge collapse in 2007.

The original Tacoma Narrows Bridge, which opened to traffic on July 1, 1940, was designed by Leon Moisseiff as a suspension bridge across Puget Sound in Washington State. Intended for both commercial and military use, the bridge took over two years to build. The bridge involved a structural plate girder that trapped wind, rather than allowing it to pass through. Toward the end of construction, workers noticed that the bridge had a tendency to bounce up and down in a wavelike motion. Apparently, this was not considered dangerous or problematic, and the bridge, informally dubbed "Galloping Gertie," opened to the public on schedule.

It had an extremely short life. On the fateful day of November 7, 1940, only four months after it opened, the bridge began to sway and oscillate violently. Concrete and steel snapped from the stresses, and the bridge soon collapsed. Miraculously, no one was killed as people had time to exit their cars and flee to safety before the bridge gave way.

The Cause of the Collapse

Several design problems factored into the collapse of the Tacoma Narrows Bridge. The plate girders were essentially solid lengths of steel-encased concrete, rather than open steel trusses. The idea was that wind would pass above and below the deck surface. However, the bridge showed a distinct tendency to oscillate along its length as wind speed increased. On November 7, winds of only 35 miles per hour (56 kilometers per hour) excited the bridge's longitudinal vibration, which caused it to oscillate with an amplitude of nearly 1.5 feet (0.5 meters).

To understand the physics behind what happened to the bridge, consider first that a wave is any sort of vibration, or disturbance, that propagates, or travels, through an object or space. Picture a wave traveling across the ocean: the ocean surface rises and falls as the energy of the wave travels through the water. Several different parameters describe a wave. The amplitude is the maximum amount of deflection, or disturbance, in one cycle of the wave. In the case of an ocean wave, the amplitude would be the distance from the trough at the bottom of one wave to the crest at the top of the next. The length of the wave, or the wave-

The parameters that describe a wave include crest (the top of the wave), trough (the bottom of the wave), and total amplitude (the distance between the wave's crest and trough).

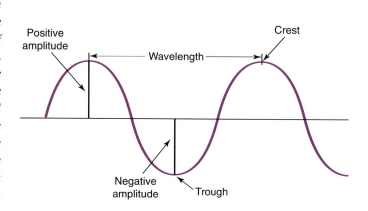

length, is the distance between two sequential wave peaks. Phase velocity is the speed at which the wave travels.

Resonance is the tendency of any object to oscillate with high amplitude at a particular vibration frequency. All objects have their own natural resonance frequency, or the vibration speed at which maximum deflections at high amplitude result. Wavelength, frequency, and speed are related by the following equation:

$$Frequency = speed/wavelength$$

The real trouble for the Tacoma Narrows Bridge began when the wind speeds increased to 42 miles per hour (68 kilometers per hour). The increased stress caused one of the suspension cables to break, and the bridge began oscillating off balance, with a twisting motion. This oscillation led to an amplitude of 28 feet (8.5 meters). Once the bridge entered this so-called torsional vibration, it essentially acted as two separate objects that were vibrating out of phase. Each half of the bridge was rotating in a different direction. As a result, a 600-foot (182-meter) span of the bridge ripped away from the suspender cables and fell into Puget Sound. More sections of the bridge would follow, leaving little remaining when the destruction was finally over. A redesigned bridge opened ten years

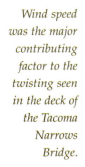

Wind speed was the major contributing factor to the twisting seen in the deck of the Tacoma Narrows Bridge.

WIND FORCE

Why did the Tacoma Narrows Bridge actually fall? Was it because of resonance alone? In short, no. In order for the bridge to shatter by virtue of resonating at its natural frequency, it would have required a constant source of excitement (wind). Wind speeds vary, so while wind turbulence was indeed a contributing factor, it was not the only one. The most plausible explanation is a combination of resonance and aerodynamic instability, which is any nonstable state caused by wind.

later. The new design included open trusses, which allowed for the through-passage of air, as well as additional bracing that had not been present in the original design.

SCHOHARIE CREEK THRUWAY BRIDGE

The Schoharie Creek Thruway Bridge collapsed without warning on April 5, 1987, after more than three decades of service. The bridge, built by the New York State Thruway Authority, spanned a distance of 540 feet (164 meters). The design incorporated four piers: two set on footings in the Schoharie Creek and one on each bank. The bridge was built in five sections measuring about 100 feet (30 meters) each, with concrete frames between the piers. Each pier frame consisted of columns held together by a plinth, or a reinforced concrete slab, which served as a base. Steel girders with steel beams running perpendicular to them made up the deck. The bridge was completed and opened for business in 1954.

Within the first year, engineers noticed cracks developing in the plinths. The columns exerted a tension force onto the plinth and, because the columns were tapered and offset, the plinth had an unacceptably high bending force exerted onto it. More steel reinforcement was added in 1957 to enable the concrete to offset these higher shear stresses. However, it was impossible to integrate the steel into the plinth without also replacing the support columns, so the plinths continued to suffer from excessive stresses.

In spring 1987, the Schoharie Creek flooded, which is not entirely unusual for a creek in springtime! Unfortunately, the weakened bridge was not up to the challenge. Pier 3 was the first to collapse, sending spans 3 and 4 down into the creek. Pier 2 collapsed about ninety minutes later. There were few cars on the bridge at the time, but ten people lost their lives as five vehicles crashed into the river.

Source of Failure

Engineers later determined that the main culprit in the collapse of pier 3 was excessive scour. Scour occurs when erosion removes sediment from the bed of a creek or stream. If too much sediment is removed from the base of the footings, they become unstable. Typical design methods for avoiding scour damage include deep footings and additional piers to help support the bridge.

Since the bridge footings were relatively shallow, it is possible that the footings simply did not extend deep enough to avoid erosion, which loosened their position in the creek bed. In addition, the fact that scour was determined to be a cause

The Schoharie Creek Thruway Bridge, located in New York State, failed in 1987 when the creek underneath it flooded.

indicates that the footings were placed in soil that was prone to erosion. A solution might have been to support the bridge using piles, or long columns driven deep into the soil, which would have provided a more stable foundation for the rest of the bridge.

TAY BRIDGE

The Tay Bridge collapse was one of the more colossal failures of a cast-iron bridge. Designed by engineer Thomas Bouch, this railway bridge was built as a cast- and wrought-iron lattice grid that spanned the Scottish Firth of Tay. The span length was considerable, nearly 2 miles (3.2 kilometers), and the bridge was constructed in eighty-five interconnected spans, each about 88 feet (27 meters) above water. The bridge was completed in 1878.

The first version of this bridge did not last long. A massive storm on December 28, 1879, with winds at 70 miles per hour (113 kilometers per hour) caused the center section of the bridge to collapse. The train that was crossing the bridge at the time fell into the bay, killing everyone onboard.

Cast-iron bridges, such as the Tay Bridge in Scotland, have failed due to connections that did not allow the structure any flexibility, or room to move, under load conditions. The bridge is seen here before it collapsed.

The Tay Bridge is shown in an artist's rendition after its 1879 collapse.

One of the main causes of the bridge's failure was in the cast-iron columns that supported the middle spans. The lugs used to connect the columns to the lateral bracing had been manufactured as part of the columns, leaving no flexibility in that part of the structure. When wind forces pushed against the columns, they were unable to deflect stress and, as a result, simply broke. Bouch had designed the bridge to withstand wind forces of 10 pounds per square foot (50 kilograms per square meter), but the storm brought considerably stronger wind forces.

If this mistake seems like an obvious miscalculation, it may well have been. Structural engineering on this scale was a relatively new field in the late nineteenth century, and in the days before detailed computer simulations, designers had to learn by trial and error. The bridge was replaced by a two-track railway bridge in 1887. The replacement used concrete and brick, in addition to steel and iron, for a more stable, load-resistant bridge.

FALLS VIEW BRIDGE

One of the first major bridges to be destroyed by ice was the Falls View (also called the Upper Steel Arch) Bridge, which spanned the Niagara River and connected Niagara Falls, New York, to Niagara Falls, Ontario. The bridge, engineered by Leffert Buck, was built in 1897 as a steel-trussed arch bridge. The main element of the superstructure was a latticed, double-hinged arch that created a very elegant design. It was, ironically, designed to replace a bridge that had previously collapsed in the same location. Buck's design was the fourth bridge to occupy this site.

The Falls View Bridge had a track for trolley cars and originally accommodated horse-drawn carriages and foot traffic. Winds in the gorge were extremely strong, and the bridge had a tendency to sway to the point where pedestrians had to hold onto the sides in order to keep from being blown off. Like its predecessors, the Falls View Bridge had a timber deck that became very slippery when it was both wet and cold—in later years at least one motorcyclist applied the brakes while on the deck and ended up skidding off into the gorge.

The Falls View Bridge, in Niagara Falls, New York, was felled by ice in 1938.

The Oakland Bay Bridge collapsed in 1989 following an earthquake in the San Francisco area, and was rebuilt. Part of it was subsequently damaged in 2007 after a gasoline tanker truck crashed and ignited. The heat from the fire actually melted an overpass leading to the bridge.

During one of the coldest periods of 1899, ice collected around the bridge abutments, reaching a height of 80 feet (24 meters). The density of water is 62 pounds per cubic foot (1 gram per cubic centimeter); the density of ice is slightly less than 1 gram, because frozen water weighs less than the liquid form. The steel used in the abutments and arch actually bent in places from the weight of all that ice, but the bridge survived this onslaught from the elements. Once summer arrived, workers constructed walls around the abutments to try to shield them from being encased in ice in the future.

In 1938, the ice struck again, this time with disastrous results. A massive storm brought huge chunks of ice from Lake Erie. Ice literally clogged the Niagara River and pushed into the bridge abutments with increasing force, causing the arch hinges to fail. While the bridge remained standing for several days afterward, the bridge span eventually disconnected and fell into the gorge. Fortunately, there was enough warning of the impending collapse that the bridge was closed to traffic and no one was harmed in the cave-in, though thousands of people watched its demise safely from both banks of the river. This bridge was later replaced by another steel-arched bridge, the Rainbow Bridge, which is still in use today.

GLOSSARY

Abutment—the portion of a bridge that supports the ends of the span; in an arched bridge, abutments are used to control the horizontal thrust of the arch

Active illumination—illumination created by lights positioned to shine directly on an object

Aerodynamic instability—any nonstable state caused by wind

Aesthetic—an artistic principle or way of describing beauty

Amplitude—the maximum amount of deflection, or disturbance, in one cycle of a wave

Antoninus Pius—Roman emperor, 138–161 C.E.

Approach—in bridge design, the portions of road leading up to the actual bridge

Aqueduct—a large structure containing a series of arches, used in the transport of water in ancient societies

Arch—a curved segment that typically spans over a door or other opening in a wall

Archimedes' Principle—a scientific maxim that states that the buoyancy force exerted on an object floating in liquid equals the weight of the fluid displaced by that object

Axial force—a force that acts along the longitudinal axis of a particular structural member

Baluster—a small vertical support used in everything from chairs to staircase railings to bridge barriers

Beam bridge—a horizontal beam laid on top of piers at either end

Bearing—a component that helps to transfer loads from the deck down to the foundation and substructure

Bending—the sagging in the middle of a beam that is caused by an excessive lateral force

Box girder—a type of beam whose components is shaped like a box; consists of two flanges and two webs

Buoyancy—an upward force exerted on any object that has been immersed in a fluid such as water

Cable-stayed bridge—a bridge that, like the suspension bridge, uses towers and cables to support the deck; inclined cables are most often used

Caisson—massive foundation that is sunk into the water until it reaches bedrock, or the lowest point of the riverbed

Camber—the positive (upward) curve that is designed into bridges, and into most beams designed for roadwork

Cantilever bridge—a bridge whose ends are anchored, but whose central span is unanchored

Cement—a binding agent used to stick objects together; usually made of lime, iron oxide, and silica; is one ingredient commonly found in concrete and mortar

Compression—a force that applies pressure to the body being acted upon, causing it to become smaller or denser

Contour intervals—the height difference between two contours on a topographic map

Creep—the regular settlement of loose dirt and other earth materials

Cross-section—the two-dimensional shape of a slice through the center of an object; for example, the cross-section of a cylinder is a circle if sliced from side to side, or a rectangle if sliced from end to end; a thicker cross-section can contribute to the overall stability of a structural form

Deck truss—in bridge design, a truss located below the bridge deck

Density—the mass per unit volume of an object

Dissipate—to spread out and travel in various directions

Drawbridge—a bridge with a deck that can rise up to allow nautical traffic to pass underneath

Dredging—digging out the bottom of a body of water, usually by removing mud and other material

Dynamic load—load that changes and can come from different directions at different times

Erosion—the gradual disintegration of earth or rock from forces such as water and wind

Falsework—full-scale wooden forms used in the creation of masonry bridges

Flange—the horizontal portions of an I-beam section

Footing—masonry connection of a bridge into the water or earth

Ford—a portion of a river that is shallow enough to be crossed on foot

Frequency—the vibration speed at which high-amplitude maximum deflections result

Friction—the force opposing the motion of two objects that are pushed past each other

Girder—a horizontal structural piece of material, such as a beam, that supports loads on a bridge or other structure

Global positioning system—a tool that provides latitude, longitude, and altitude information

Glulam beam—a composite wood beam made by several layers of wood being glued together, under pressure, with structurally sound adhesive

Guardrail—a railing that is built along the edge of the bridge deck; prevents people and cars from falling off the edge of the bridge

Hew—to cut with an axe

I-beam—a type of girder consisting of a vertical piece called a web, and two horizontal members called flanges on either end

Igneous rock—rock that was formed by hardened melted material, such as volcanic material

Industrialization—the process of a society's transition from agricultural to manufactured output

Keystone—a wedge-shaped piece of stone or other material that sits at the very top of an arch and helps keep the other stones in their proper position

Latex concrete—concrete (sand, cement, and aggregate rock) mixed with latex and water

Light pollution—any illumination, usually in the night sky, that comes from artificial sources of light such as lamps and streetlights

Load—that which must be supported by a bridge; includes both static loads, such as the weight of the bridge and its fixtures, and live loads, such as the weight of traffic and pressure due to wind

Load-bearing masonry—stone or brick that, when formed into a wall, supports the weight above it in addition to its own weight

Long-span bridge—a bridge that requires extra piers to be placed somewhere in the middle

Median barrier—an obstruction that helps separate traffic flowing in opposite directions

Metamorphic rock—rock that has been created or changed by heat or pressure

Midspan—occurring in the middle of a road or bridge section

Passive illumination—illumination created through light reflecting off reflective paint or some other reflective material

Permanent load—a load that is always present and acting upon a structure; includes the weight of all materials

Phase velocity—the speed at which a wave travels

Pier—vertical masonry that transfers loads from one point to another; often used in bridge and arch construction

Pile—long vertical objects that are driven into the soil, usually to serve as supports

Pin joint—a joint where members are attached using a pin that can rotate

Plinth—concrete slab, usually to prevent wood or other materials from coming into direct contact with earth

Pontoon—a floating, buoyant object (such as a boat) whose purpose is to support a weight

Post-tensioning—a method of structural strengthening that involves steel rods being placed into a concrete beam's mold unstretched; these rods are stretched, usually by hydraulic machinery, after the concrete has been poured and hardened

Prestressing—applying tension to a beam or other building material to counteract the forces that are imposed once the beam is placed into its final position

Pylon—in bridge design, a large vertical structural element used in cable-stayed bridges

Resonance—the tendency of any object to oscillate with high amplitude at a particular built-in vibration frequency

Scour—a condition that occurs when sediment is removed from a creekbed or streambed due to erosion

Sea level—the height of the ocean's surface taken as an average between low and high tide

Sedimentary rock—rock that is made of sediment, or multiple layers, usually deposited in an aquatic environment

Shear stress—a state created by parallel planes sliding against each other

Short-span bridge—a bridge that requires only abutments at either end

Signage—a system or series of signs

Sluice—a type of gate equipped with a valve, used to allow water to flow through an aqueduct or other device

Span—in bridge design, the distance between piers or supports

Stable configuration—in bridge design, a truss system that will not collapse under pressure

Static load—a load that remains constant over time

Suspension bridge—a bridge that uses towers and cables to support the weight of the deck

Temporary load—a load that changes over time, and may or may not be present depending on conditions

Tension—a force that acts to stretch the body being acted upon

Thermal changes—any change in weather or temperature conditions

Through truss—in bridge design, a truss located above the bridge deck

Topographic mapping—creating a map of any three-dimensional surface; topographic maps show three-dimensional information

Torsion—a twisting force

Traffic barrier—an obstruction that helps separate traffic that flows in opposite directions; usually positioned to help separate pedestrian and road traffic

Transfer—the tendency of loads to move to areas that can better handle them

Truss—a framework of beams that is shaped to form a rigid structure

Truss bridge—a bridge whose structural system is designed around one or more large trusses

Uplift—a type of force that is exerted vertically upward

Voussoir—a sloping, wedge-shaped piece of stone or other material that makes up an arch

Wave—any sort of vibration, or disturbance, that propagates through an object or space

Wavelength—the distance between two sequential peaks of a wave

Web—the vertical portion of an I-beam section

FIND OUT MORE

Books

Peters, Tom F. *Transitions in Engineering: Guillaume Henri Dufour and the Early 19th Century Cable Suspension Bridges.* Boston: Birkhauser Verlag, 1987.

Petroski, Henry. *Engineers of Dreams: Great Bridge Builders and the Spanning of America.* New York: Knopf, 1995.

Scott, Richard. *In the Wake of Tacoma: Suspension Bridges and the Quest for Aerodynamic Stability.* Reston, VA: American Society of Civil Engineers, 2001.

Ward-Perkins, John B. *Roman Architecture.* New York: Electa/Rizzoli, 1988.

Whitney, Charles S. *Bridges of the World: Their Design and Construction.* Mineola, NY: Dover, 2003.

Web sites

The American Institute of Physics
    www.aip.org

The American Society of Civil Engineers
    www.pubs.asce.org

Building Big: Bridges. In particular, check out the "Bridge Challenge."
    www.pbs.org/wgbh/buildingbig/bridge/index.html

Georgia State University Physics Department
    http://hyperphysics.phy-astr.gsu.edu/hbase/hframe.html
    (Go to http://hyperphysics.phy-astr.gsu.edu/hbase/pflu.html#fp
    for information on static fluid pressure.)

Glenbrook South School Physics Classroom
    www.glenbrook.k12.il.us/gbssci/Phys/Class/BBoard.html
Golden Gate Bridge Official Web Site
    www.goldengatebridge.org
NASA's Glenn Learning Technologies Project
    www.lerc.nasa.gov/WWW/K-12
Science and Technology Museum
    Background information for "Structures and Shapes"
    www.sciencetech.technomuses.ca/english/schoolzone/Info_structures.cfm
Symphonies in Steel:
    Bay Bridge and the Golden Gate
    www.sfmuseum.org/hist9/mcgloin.html
U.S. Department of Transportation Federal Highway Administration
    www.fhwa.dot.gov
The Virtual Museum of the City of San Francisco
    www.sfmuseum.org/hist10/ggbridging.html

INDEX

Page numbers in italics refer to illustrations.